ROUTLEDGE LIBRARY EDITIONS:
BUSINESS CYCLES

Volume 3

CYCLICAL PRODUCTIVITY IN U.S. MANUFACTURING

CYCLICAL PRODUCTIVITY IN U.S. MANUFACTURING

MIGUEL JIMÉNEZ

First published in 1997

This edition first published in 2015
by Routledge
2 Park Square, Milton Park, Abingdon, Oxon, OX14 4RN

and by Routledge
711 Third Avenue, New York, NY 10017

Routledge is an imprint of the Taylor & Francis Group, an informa business

British Library Cataloguing in Publication Data
A catalogue record for this book is available from the British Library

ISBN: 978-1-138-85286-0 (Set)
eISBN: 978-1-315-71360-1 (Set)
ISBN: 978-1-138-85827-5 (Volume 3)
eISBN: 978-1-315-71814-9 (Volume 3)

CYCLICAL PRODUCTIVITY IN U.S. MANUFACTURING

MIGUEL JIMÉNEZ

GARLAND PUBLISHING, INC.
NEW YORK & LONDON / 1997

Library of Congress Cataloging-in-Publication Data

Jiménez, Miguel, 1965–
Cyclical productivity in U.S. manufacturing / Miguel Jiménez.
p. cm. — (Garland studies on industrial productivity)
Includes bibliographical references and index.
ISBN 0-8153-2974-1 (alk. paper)
1. Industrial productivity. 2. Industrial productivity—United States. 3. Business cycles. 4. Externalities (Economics) 5. Labor turnover I. Title. II. Series.
HD56.J56 1997
338.5'42'0973—dc21 97-37066

Printed on acid-free, 250-year-life paper
Manufactured in the United States of America

Contents

List of Tables

Preface

This book presents several pieces of empirical work that try to disentangle why the standard measures of productivity growth used in Macroeconomics turn out to be procyclical for American manufacturing industries. This fact has been observed not only for the manufacturing sector, and not only for the US economy. It is a regular occurrence that is recurrent for different countries and economic sectors, and as such it has to be accounted for by any theory of the business cycle that tries to give a good representation of the fluctuations of the main economic aggregates.

As we will see in the text, traditional Keynesian theories of the cycle do not explain satisfactorily why productivity is procyclical, whereas the new Real Business Cycle theories developed since the beginning of the 80s by John Prescott, Finn Kydland and other authors give a natural explanation of this behavior. Productivity grows more in expansions, they argue, because economic growth is driven by improvements in technology. Periods when innovations are introduced in the economic activity are those in which the economy grows more. The force of technology for generating economic cycles is much more important than that of the management or mismanagement of monetary or fiscal policies, as Keynesians and monetarists argued in the 50s and the 60s.

Although the influence of Real Business Cycle theories on macroeconomic modelling has been impressive, many economists feel uncomfortable with the idea that technology shocks drive the cycle. On the one hand, the magnitude of those shocks in order to account for actual output fluctuations is implausibly large. On the other hand, direct evidence of a cyclical pattern for innovations is by no means clear. Therefore, some alternative theories for procyclical productivity growth have been put forward in recent years. The main thrust in all of them is how to explain why the

Solow residual, which is the most frequently used aggregate measure of productivity growth, is positive in economic booms while true technology growth is not especially large in those periods. The assessment of these alternative theories is the main topic of my research.

The existence of markup pricing (prices above the marginal cost), production externalities (improvements in the productivity of a firm due to the interaction with other firms) and labor hoarding or variations in effort over the cycle are the three alternatives studied in recent literature. This book dedicates a chapter to each of them, without reaching a clear conclusion about which of them explains the data best. Labor hoarding and effort variations (what I call *slow adjustment in the labor input*) seem to play a role in the movements of the Solow residual, but markup pricing and externalities are also very important. Unfortunately, it is not very clear which of these two is prevalent, since both of them seem to explain the same type of correlations in the data. However, I hope it will be clear at the end of the book that theories that rely on technology shocks have good competitors in explaining the cyclical behavior of measured productivity growth.

The methodology used in this study is heavily indebted to several authors that have previously examined this topic. Chapter 3 uses Robert Hall's original method to estimate markups and extends it to the dual version of the Solow residual. A similar extension has been used by Werner Roeger in an article published when I was finishing my research. His method is somewhat different from mine and does not depend on instrumental variables estimation, although, in my opinion, it obscures the relationship between markups and the sources of business cycles. Chapter 4 (which was written in collaboration with Domenico Marchetti, now at the Bank of Italy) and Chapter 5 use a Vector Autoregressive model that is based on the work of Argia Sbordone, whereas the idea of externalities producing procyclical Solow residuals was originally developed by Ricardo Caballero and Richard Lyons. Several articles by Susanto Basu, John Fernald and other researchers that have carried out very careful work on the same kind of data that have been used here have also influenced the way I (and Domenico Marchetti in Chapter 4) have treated the data.

The work presented here fits not only within the field of empirical Macroeconomics, but also within that of Industrial Economics, since as a by-product an estimation of markups for several manufacturing industries in the US is presented. Although estimations with aggregated data are not completely accepted by industrial economists, the database used in this case (developed by Wayne Gray) is disaggregated up to four-digit level in the SIC industrial classification. These data should give more accurate estimations, and I hope they will contribute to establishing some link between both disciplines, which very often ignore each other completely.

Acknowledgments

This book was written as a PhD dissertation at the European University Institute in Florence, Italy. Working in Florence was a very pleasant experience, as the reader can imagine. I want to thank the Institute in the first place for giving me the opportunity of working in the Badia for such a long time. The Institute of Fiscal Studies, in Spain, also gave me financial support for more than one year. But the main support I have received has been intellectual, and in that respect Robert Waldmann deserves all my gratitude. Not only has he given me excellent advice, but he has also shown me the excitement of intellectual work while I was trying to follow him in our two-hour conversations in his office. I also thank him for the enormous patience he has shown with my work throughout all this time. Domenico Marchetti has co-authored chapter 4 of this book, and has also encouraged me in the writing of all the computer programs that I have used in the other papers. He has provided me with the data, although I think in this case Eric Bartelsmann at the Federal Reserve was our main source. Fabio Canova read an early version of chapter 4 and made useful suggestions. Juan F. Jimeno and Samuel Bentolila proposed a number of corrections and additions to the three main chapters of the book. Ide Kearney helped me a lot trying to polish my English in an early version of the book, although I am afraid that new re-writings after her collaboration have spoiled her work.

All those friends who made me have a great time in Florence know how much I thank them, and that because of them I will never forget my stay at the EUI. I also want to mention the support of my family and especially my parents. Finally, I dedicate this book to Beatriz Aparicio, who was born exactly one year before I finished writing it.

Cyclical Productivity in U.S. Manufacturing

1

Explanations of cyclical productivity growth

1.1 Procyclical Productivity

The development of (RBC) theories in the 1980's produced a radical shift in the explanation of the source of economic fluctuations. In traditional Keynesian models, cycles originate from changes in exogenous demand (government expenditure, money supply, etc.) and are propagated through the imperfect functioning of different markets (especially the labor and money markets). These imperfections produce a suboptimal level of employment and output, which makes fluctuations undesiderable and their reduction a legitimate goal of economic policy. RBC models assume instead that the real economy works in an analogous way to a perfectly competitive general equilibrium economy. Shocks to technology, propagating through the intertemporal substitution of leisure and labor, are considered the main source of business cycles (at least in the early versions of these models). Because markets are competitive, fluctuations are the optimal adaptation to the new technology conditions and no intervention is needed. Economic cycles are efficient. These differing views make the identification of the source of business cycles a key policy question.

There are two main reasons for the success of RBC models. First, the simulated versions of highly simplified models reproduce the comovements of actual macroeconomic variables relatively well. Second, by imposing a positive correlation between the cycle and technology, they give an explanation for the observed procyclicality of standard measures of productivity. This is one of the facts that traditional Keynesian models found more difficult to explain, because any theory which assumes that firms are always on a fixed downward sloping labor demand curve will yield countercyclical real wages and labor productivity.

The behavior of productivity over the cycle is thus a key issue in testing these two competitive theories of the cycle. The Solow residual (SR)[1] is the classical measure of multifactor productivity growth. It is defined as follows:

$$SR = (y - k) - S_N(n - k) - S_M(m - k)$$

where y, n, m and k are, respectively, the growth rates of output, labor, intermediate materials and capital, and S_N and S_M are the revenue shares of labor and materials. The procyclicality of the SR has been cited as evidence in support of the validity of RBC models.[2]

However, the assertion that the SR correctly measures changes in productivity depends critically on the correct measurement of variables and on two crucial assumptions, namely constant returns to scale and perfect competition in the output and input markets. These assumptions are very controversial for changes in productivity at high frequencies. Once it is accepted that the SR is procyclical, the problem of testing for procyclical technological progress is equivalent to testing jointly for perfect competition, constant returns to scale and the correct measurement of variables. Departures from any or all of these assumptions result in several alternative explanations for procyclical SR. The analysis of the possible failure of these assumptions is the main objective of this book.

In the next two sections we give a description of these three alternative explanations of procyclical productivity growth, presented from the perspective of the debate that has taken place in the literature on the matter.

1.2 Imperfect Competition and Labor Hoarding

The standard Keynesian explanation of procyclical SR rests on the assumption of labor hoarding. In recessions, firms do not lay off redundant workers because they face some adjustment costs. The reduction in demand and output is not followed by a reduction in labor input, but rather by a reduction in its utilization, leading to a spurious negative SR. In the formula above this corresponds to a negative y and a zero n. Thus the SR fails to measure true productivity changes because of the slow adjustment of the labor input, and instead measures fluctuations in demand.[3]

In a famous paper, *Robert Hall (1988)* proposes a new explanation for the correlation of measured productivity with aggregate activity. He shows how the procyclical behavior of the SR can be explained by firms pricing their output at a markup on marginal cost. This implies that one of the implicit assumptions of the SR (perfect competition) is not fulfilled. His argument goes as follows. If prices are higher than marginal cost then the revenue share of factors other than capital will undervalue the elasticity of production with respect to inputs, and therefore the SR will overestimate true productivity changes in expansions and underestimate them in recessions, increasing their procyclicality. In the formula above, S_N will not reflect the true contribution of labor to production. Similarly, under increasing returns the sum of the elasticities of output with respect to all factors of production is bigger than one. These elasticities will be underestimated by the revenue shares, since prices must be higher than marginal cost to prevent bankruptcy.

Hall shows that the SR is correlated with instruments of demand, and interprets this result as a failure of competition. He then calculates the level of markups that would explain such a correlation for 26 two-digit SIC[4] US manufacturing industries, and finds very high values. (The data he uses do not include intermediate inputs, since they are taken from the National Income and Product Accounts (NIPA)). The estimation of markups is linked to the idea that they explain all the cyclical behavior of the SR. To reconcile these high markups with the absence of large profits in those industries he suggests that markups compensate chronic excess capacity or increasing returns to scale. Interestingly, he shows that, in the absence of effort variation, costs of adjusting labor input cannot be taken as a plausible explanation for procyclical SR if there are no markups. This is because, under competition, if firms hoard labor then marginal cost and prices will fall enough to compensate the underutilization of capital thereby offsetting the reduction in output. Thus labor hoarding is not likely to be an independent explanation of procyclical SR.

In a subsequent paper (*Hall, 1990*) he derives a version of the SR which weights inputs with cost shares instead of revenue shares. Cost-based SRs measure productivity correctly even under imperfect competition; however, the fact that this measure is still correlated with demand suggests that increasing returns (the second failure of Solow's assumptions) are a key explanation of the procyclical SR and of high markups.

In brief, Hall claims that markups are a key element in explaining procyclical productivity. Increasing returns and labor hoarding are also important, but they cannot on their own explain the positive correlation of the Solow Residual with demand. In particular, the lack of substantial profits suggests that markups are closely connected with the increasing returns explanation.

Subsequent to Hall's work, a series of articles have tried to disentangle in the same line of research what is behind the movements of the Solow residual. One strand of the discussion has tried to re-estimate markups and returns to scale with gross output instead of value-added data (recall that Hall used value-added data). The reason for this is that value-added data produce biased estimates of the parameters of interest when there is imperfect competition, because in this case value added changes as calculated by standard double-deflation methods are not correct. These are some of the contributions:

Waldmann (1991) points out that the double-deflation method is not used in all manufacturing industries, and that other dubious criteria for measuring value added produce implausibly high markups for some sectors. These incorrect calculations of value added lead to an apparent markup since the bias is correlated with demand.

Norrbin (1993) extends Hall's dataset to include intermediate inputs and reapplies Hall's markup estimations. He finds that the inclusion of materials reduces considerably the level of markups (to about 10%), and that they are only marginally statistically significant. He also uses corroborative evidence from another data set which includes intermediate inputs (developed by Jorgenson et al. (1987), covering two-digit SIC manufacturing industries[5]) and obtain similar results.

In a paper by *Basu and Fernald (1994)* it is shown how the bias in the construction of value-added data affects the estimation of increasing returns to scale. They use Jorgenson's data set, and apply Hall's method to estimate the degree of returns to scale using both gross output and value-added regressions. In both cases they find roughly constant returns to scale. They also show how double-deflation methods for constructing value-added figures (as opposed to the preferred Divisia index method) explain the high values which Hall found.

Domowitz et al. (1988) find that the level of markups is still very high even using a data set that includes gross output and materials. Furthermore, the level of disaggregation is very high (four-digit SIC sectors). They conclude that the very large values estimated by Hall for some sectors are due to the exclusion of intermediate inputs from NIPA series, but that markups are significant and large for most manufacturing industries even using gross output-based Solow residuals. In Chapter 2 we will see that a possible undermeasurement of the materials share in their data and in that which we use may partially explain the difference between these results and the ones obtained by Norrbin (1993) and Basu and Fernald (1994).

A different direction of the debate focussed on the identification of other causes of procyclical SR that can be complementary to or substitutes for the markups explanation and which can help explain the observed lack of substantial pure profits in manufacturing. One possibility, already mentioned, is labor hoarding. Although it does not affect the SR if firms are competitive, it is possible that semi-fixed labor input together with countercyclical markups result in cyclical measured productivity. This is exactly what happens in *Rotemberg and Summers (1990)* model. With rigid prices labor hoarding produces procyclical productivity, since rigid prices imply countercyclical markups when marginal cost moves with demand.

Overhead labor is considered the key element that compensates price-cost margins in Domowitz et al. (1988). In general, overhead workers are more of a fixed factor than production workers, and this fixity can explain the low profitability that accompanies high markups. *Morrison (1992)* carefully models semi-fixed labor and capital in a dynamic optimization setting using aggregate manufacturing data. She adopts a structural approach with a fairly sophisticated cost function that allows for variable utilization of semi-fixed factors over the cycle to account for countercyclical markups.

More recent papers have concentrated on the role of cyclical utilization of capital as a possible explanation of procyclical SR. The logic is similar to that of labor hoarding, but applied in this case to capital instead of labor: measures of capital do not reflect its true contribution to production. Burnside et al. (1995) and Burnside (1996) present some evidence in this sense and find that returns to scale are constant. Basu (1996) takes materials use as a proxy of capacity utilization and argues that a mixture of capital and labor cyclical utilization rates reduces greatly the size of true technology shocks.

In sum, the main contribution of Hall's work is its originality, by giving a new interpretation to the behavior of the SR. New articles show that the actual size of markups depends very much on the quality of the data, since measurement errors in inputs' shares and the contribution of labor produce different results. In this sense, the possibility of working with a very disaggregated data set seems a clear advantage of our investigation.

1.3 Externalities

Another possible explanation for procyclical SR is external increasing returns to scale. External economies have played an important role in recent theoretical models of the business cycle[6], and they are a possible source of multiple equilibria. From an empirical point of view, the most successful attempt to estimate the degree of externalities at a sectoral level is the article by *Caballero and Lyons (1992)*, who use two-digit SIC NIPA data[7] with an approach very similar to that of Hall. With cost-based input shares (as in Hall's 1990 study), they calculate the degree of returns to scale at different levels of aggregation showing that returns to scale are lower at industry level than for the whole manufacturing sector. The obvious explanation of this observation is that economies of scale are internalized at higher levels of aggregation because of thick markets effects or other kind of externalities. In *Caballero and Lyons (1990)* they also find evidence of external returns to scale in the industrial sectors of several European countries.

Their results have been criticized on the grounds of the data they use, as in the case of the estimation of markups. The reliability of external returns to scale estimations with value-added functions has been questioned by *Basu and Fernald (1995)*, who argue that they can be biased when there is not perfect competition. The reasoning is equivalent to that in Basu and Fernald (1994), when they reassess Hall's estimations of internal increasing returns. They also point out that Caballero and Lyons' finding of externalities relies partly on significant *decreasing* returns to scale at the firm level, which they argue are implausible. However, *Bartelsmann, Caballero and Lyons (1994)* re-estimate their model with the same data set which we use in this study (which includes materials inputs) and still obtain an important degree of externalities.

1.4 The Dual Approach

Another way of utilizing the behavior of productivity to identify the sources of business cycles is given in *Shapiro (1987)*, where he uses the dual approach to derive an alternative measure of productivity growth, the dual Solow residual (DSR), which is based on the prices of output and inputs instead of the quantities. Following Summers (1986), who criticizes RBC models for not testing their implications for prices, Shapiro shows that his price-based measure of productivity must equal the SR under perfect competition and constant returns to scale, since under these assumptions both measures capture true productivity change well. Shapiro claims that the high correlation he finds between both measures implies that it is difficult to reject the hypotheses of competition and constant returns, and that this result supports RBC theories. He argues that Keysenian theories can explain the procyclical behavior of the SR, but not its comovement with the DSR. The reason for this is that under competition and constant returns to scale factor prices will move only if their true productivity changes, but not if there is labor hoarding, price-cost margins or externalities.

As we will see, one of the main points of our research is to give alternative interpretations of procyclical DSR that rely on demand or materials shocks for explaining the business cycle. We will extend the arguments of biased SR to the DSR and will stress the role played by explanations other than improvements in technology. Both residuals will be used for the estimation of markups, in a similar way to the one *Roeger (1995)* uses, but with a different interpretation.

1.5 Plan of the Book

In this study we present evidence on the ability of two different explanations, namely, price-cost margins and externalities, to account for procyclical measured productivity. Chapter 3 is devoted to the estimation of markups, whereas Chapter 4 deals with the estimation of the degree of external returns to scale. Both explanations are connected in that they depend on demand shocks or materials price shocks as the force which drives the cycle, in contrast to the RBC tradition, where the SR correctly measures the technology shocks that drive economic fluctuations.

In both chapters we will see that labor hoarding and effort variations may also play a role in driving productivity measures, although not as important as that of markups and externalities, and in any case not independently of these two. In Chapter 5 we look more in detail at the effects of slow adjustment of labor on the SR and the DSR.

In Chapter 3, we use information from the dual Solow residual to estimate markups and compare these with the ones obtained with the SR. Shapiro maintains that the positive correlation of the SR with the DSR cannot be explained by changes in demand. However we argue that the correlation between the SR and the DSR need not imply procyclical technology change. We will show that a procyclical DSR can be produced by materials' price shocks and markups if increases in materials prices are correlated with recessions. Therefore we can reconcile Shapiro's finding with a combination of imperfect competition, markups and both demand and energy price shocks (taking into account that both types of shocks are highly correlated in our sample period). Furthermore, the DSR can be reinterpreted by relaxing the assumptions of competition and constant returns, in the same way Hall does with the SR, and so the DSR can also be used to calculate markups and an index of returns to scale. This is done using an instrumental variables estimator. The combination of both residuals increases the robustness of the estimations, since we use information from very different variables (prices and quantities) to calculate a single parameter.

An important criticism of Hall's work (and of all econometric exercises that try to isolate aggregate demand shocks) is the choice of instruments. We try to solve this problem by testing for possible overidentification restrictions imposed by the standard aggregate instruments (i.e., growth rates of GNP, oil prices, defense expenditures and import prices) and find that for many sectors these instruments do not pass the test of overidentification. As an alternative we use, for each industry, the SR and the DSR of those sectors not related to it through input demand linkages, as suggested by *Jimeno (1989)*. These instruments should be more robust than aggregate instruments. We also test for overidentification these sectoral instruments, and retain only the SR and DSR of those sectors which pass the overidentifying test.

A similar approach to the estimation of markups has been used by Roeger (1995). He also takes account of the fact that the SR and the DSR are biased in the presence of markups. He uses information from both residuals to estimate these markups. However, his interpretation of the driving forces behind the business cycle is the direct opposite to ours, since he assumes that technology shocks are still the main force explaining procyclical SR and DSR, whereas we demonstrate that demand or oil shocks can also explain this behavior. We believe that his reasons for not considering the importance of demand shocks in driving the cycle are flawed, as we explain in Chapter 3. The main difference between our work and Roeger's is that we use the standard instrumental variables approach to identify the influence of demand on productivity measures.[8]

Chapter 4, which is joint work with Domenico Marchetti, analyzes the effect on productivity of an aggregate shock to economic activity. Using a dynamic approach, we evaluate the importance of externalities for the movements of productivity over the business cycle.

Caballero and Lyons' approach to measuring externalities cannot adequately separate the effects of labor hoarding and effort changes from true external effects. They use proxies for effort in their regressions, but these are never completely satisfactory. Rather than trying to measure effort, we follow *Sbordone's (1997)* dynamic framework to identify labor hoarding effects separately from productive externalities. The method we use can be summarized as follows. Within a vector autoregressive (VAR) model, we simulate a highly persistent innovation in aggregate activity. We investigate over time the induced change in sectoral productivity. As time passes, labor hoarding and effort variation effects die out, since the quantity of hired labor will adjust to the new level of activity, whereas "true" trading and technological externalities will persist. The detection of a persistent positive effect on the productivity level is therefore interpreted as evidence of external effects. An extension of our base model shows that our results cannot be attributed simply to oil price shocks.

In Chapter 5 we examine carefully the possibility that labor hoarding and effort variations bias the results we obtain in Chapters 3 and 4. First it is analyzed how labor hoarding and effort variations may have different effects on the DSR in the short run. However, in the long run, after slow adjustments have taken place, both types of biases will disappear. We apply the VAR model of Chapter 4 to the DSR, and compare the results obtained with those of the SR VAR. For some sectors the final level of productivity after an aggregate shock will be very close in both models, indicating that the evidence of externalities in Chapter 4 is reinforced using data on prices.

In the second part of the chapter more direct evidence on the slow adjustment of measured inputs to aggregate shocks is presented. Here we simulate the effect of the aggregate shock on sectoral output growth, labor and materials inputs. The effect on sectoral output is almost immediate and persistent. The effect on labor and materials is slower. Provided that the identifying assumptions of our model are correct, this gives definitive evidence that labor hoarding and effort variations over the cycle play an important role in the behavior of the SR in the US economy.

The panel data we use throughout the book include materials quantities and prices for all US manufacturing industries over the period 1958-84. It is very disaggregated, so it helps us avoid possible aggregation biases as well as the problems associated with value-added calculations. These data and some adjustments we have made to measure the revenue shares of the labor input correctly are explained in some detail in Chapter 2. It should be clear from the preceding literature review that a correct treatment of the data is key for obtaining accurate results.

Finally, we include an appendix that describes the programs written in MATLAB to deal with the panel data. These may be of some interest since they perform computations which cannot be easily done using standard panel data packages, like the estimation of panel VAR models and the calculation of robust standard errors for panel estimations with fixed effects and instrumental variables.

Notes

[1]Introduced for the first time in Solow (1957).

[2]See Long and Plosser (1983). They show that the unconditional joint distribution of output growth in many sectors looks very similar to that of an aggregate shock model.

[3]The idea of labor hoarding was introduced by Oi (1962). For a Real Business Cycle model that incorporates labor hoarding, see Burnside, Eichenbaum and Rebelo (1993).

[4]Standard Industrial Code.

[5]We will also use this data set in Chapter 4 to give complementary evidence of the main results we obtain there.

[6]See Kiyotaki (1988) and Murphy et al. (1989).

[7]The same data used by Hall (1988).

[8]The other difference is the data. Roeger uses the value added NIPA series, as Hall (1988) and Caballero and Lyons (1992).

2

Data

In this chapter we describe the sources of the data we use, their possible shortcomings and the necessary adjustments we have made in order to correct for these. In particular, we look at the problems in measuring correctly the revenue shares of the labor input.

2.1 Sources and Variables

The data set used throughout the book has been developed with the Annual Survey of Manufacturers and the Census of Manufacturers in the US as the main source. Both are conducted by the US Census Bureau. They cover 450 four-digit SIC (Standard Industry Classification of 1972) American manufacturing industries from 1958 to 1984, although from these we only use 402. We have omitted all those sectors included in two-digit manufacturing industry number 20, Food products, since it is a large group that includes very diverse sectors that do not show the same pattern of behavior.

Table 2.1 in the appendix presents the list of sectors included in the data set at the two-digit level. The number of four-digit sub-sectors inside each industry is also provided, since the sizes of sectors are very different. The third column gives the total value added of each two-digit sector averaged over the sample period. Column 4 includes the relative size of each sector with respect to the whole manufacturing sector (calculated with our working data, i.e. excluding Food products from the total amount).

Durable industries (numbers 24, 25, and from number 32 to 39) are larger than non-durables in the number of sub-sectors and in the quantity of recorded output. There is a core of durables sectors, numbers 32-37, that together account for 57% of value added. They correspond to intermediate goods and investment goods that are likely to be used by most other economic sectors. All durables produce, on average, 67% of the total value added of the industries under consideration.[1] Among non-durables, 26 Paper products, 27 Printing and 28 Chemicals are the largest industries.

An initial version of the data set (with data up to 1976) was developed as a joint project by the University of Pennsylvania, the Bureau of Census and SRI, Inc. It has been updated until 1986[2] by Wayne Gray at the National Bureau of Economic Research (NBER).[3]

The Annual Census of Manufacturers is used for eleven variables of the data set: number of workers, total payroll, number of production workers, number of production worker hours, total production worker wages, value of shipments, value added, inventories, new capital investment, expenditure on energy and expenditure on materials. For some other variables (capital measures and deflators for all the variables) information has been taken from several US government agencies. Special effort was dedicated to the deflator of materials, which is constructed with the help of input-output tables at a very disaggregated level.

From the 18 variables included in the data set, we use nominal output, the deflator for nominal output, real labor input and its compensation (for two different types of labor), cost of materials and its deflator, and real capital stock. They are defined as follows:

1. *Nominal gross output*: Measured as the value of industry shipments plus inventory change, in millions of dollars.

2. *Output price*: Price deflator for the value of shipments (1972=1). It is used as a proxy for the gross output deflator, since no inventory deflator is included in the data set. It comes from the Bureau of Economic Analysis (BEA) in the Commerce Department, and it is based on product price indices from the Bureau of Labor Statistics (BLS), supplemented by a few specialized deflators for military goods from the government division of the BEA. Part of the data (until 1980) is based on product price indices (seven-digit products

within each industry), and part on industry-based price indices (from 1981), created by the BLS.

3. *Total labor*: Number of employees in 1,000s. It includes workers in production plants (production and non-production workers). It does not include employees in auxiliary (administrative) units.

4. *Compensation of total labor*: Total payroll in millions of dollars without social security payments and employer payments for some fringe benefits.

5. *Production workers*: Number of production workers in thousands.

6. *Compensation of production workers*: Their wages in millions of dollars.

7. *Materials Cost*: Measured in millions of dollars. It includes energy spending, but excludes purchased services, and therefore the cost of total intermediate inputs is under-estimated.

8. *Price of materials*: Price deflator for materials (1972=1). It was constructed by averaging together price deflators for 529 inputs (corresponding to 369 manufacturing industries and 160 non-manufacturing industries), using as weights the relative size of each industry's purchases of that input in the Bureau of Census' Input-Output tables. The tables were obtained for 1972, 1977 and 1980-82.

9. *Capital*: Real capital stock in millions of 1972 dollars, including structures and equipment. They reflect capital stock measures at the beginning of the year.

The other variables which we use and which are not given directly in the data base are the ratio of nominal values over price deflators (for real gross output and real intermediate inputs) and compensation of labor divided by the quantity of labor (for wages). The share and quantities of non-production workers are derived by substracting the figures for production workers from those of total labor.

2.2 Adjustment of the Labor Share

There are two main advantages of Gray's data set with respect to the data commonly used in the literature; first, the level of disaggregation is very high, and second, it includes intermediate inputs so that it allows us to work with a gross output production function. In fact, most articles based on Hall's 1988 paper involve an extension in these two directions.

The importance of disaggregated data is easy to understand if we consider the fact that industrial economists find it difficult to believe in estimations of markups based on two-digit SIC industries.[4] The papers by Domowitz et al. (1988) and Bartelsmann, Caballero and Lyons (1994) use datasets that come from the same sources as Gray's, and they take advantage of the power that they offer for the estimation of price-cost margins or indices of externalities. In our case, the efficency of the estimations we obtain is due mainly to the fact that we use four-digit SIC data.

Several articles have discussed the inadequacy of working with value-added production functions, instead of gross-output functions, when we want to estimate the parameters involved in equations like the one derived by Hall.[5] The bias comes from the fact that value-added measures are calculated under the same assumptions used for deriving the SR, i.e. perfect competition and constant returns. But when prices are higher than marginal cost, the share of materials underestimates their contribution to final production, such that part of this contribution is attributed to value added. The underestimation can lead to a spurious SR positively correlated with materials use.[6]

A similar bias applies to the dual measure of productivity (the dual Solow residual, DSR), the one that uses prices instead of quantities. In this case, materials' price increases shift the value-added deflator up when it is calculated using revenue shares as weights, inducing a DSR negatively correlated with materials price movements. Positive oil price shocks can produce a spurious negative SR through their depressing effect on demand together with a spurious negative DSR through the positive movement of the value-added deflator. This is a possible explanation of Shapiro's (1987) finding of positive correlation of these two residuals, which is one of the issues we examine in Chapter 3.[7]

All these problems disappear if we work with a gross output function which includes material inputs. However, the data set we use has been criticized by Norrbin (1993),[8] on the grounds of a mismeasurement of labor and materials' shares, leading to an upward bias in the calculation of markups. In particular, he claims that data from the Bureau of Census and the Annual Census of Manufacturers does not include Social Security payments and some fringe benefits in measured labor compensation, and that compensation and hours worked do not include those people working in administrative units (since the census covers establishments, not firms). Also, there are some payments for services which are not included in the cost of materials. The undermeasurement of factors' shares has a similar effect on the SR and the DSR than the miscalculation of value added and value-added deflator have when prices are higher than marginal cost. Given that basically Hall's method for estimating markups consists of comparing the elasticities of the production function to the shares of inputs, undervalued shares will yield productivity growth measures spuriously correlated with output, and will thus produce an upwardly biased estimate of the markup.

In order to partially avoid this problem, we correct the measures of labor shares by multiplying the labor compensation of each four-digit industry by an adjustment factor, which is different for each two-digit sector and each time period.[9] This adjustment factor is equal to the "correct" NIPA labor compensation divided by the undervalued equivalent in our dataset.

In Chapters 3 and 5 we use a different definition of the SR than the one we use in Chapter 4. In the former two chapters we construct the SR with three inputs, i.e. capital, labor and intermediate inputs, whereas in Chapter 4 we use, apart from capital and materials, two different types of labor inputs, that is, the number of production and non-production workers (without including those in auxiliary units, as indicated above).[10] When defining two types of labor, we apply the same adjusting coefficient C_t to both types of shares (production and non-production workers):

$$C_t = \frac{COMP_{NIPA,t}}{COMP_{CENSUS,t}} \tag{2.1}$$

where $COMP_{NIPA,t}$ is the compensation of labor in period t correctly calculated by the National Income and Product Accounts

(NIPA) figures at the two-digit level, and $COMP_{CENSUS,t}$ is the sum over four-digit industries within each two-digit sector of the variable "*Compensation of total labor*" in our panel, also at period t. This latter figure underestimates the real compensation because it includes neither the wages of those people employed in administrative units nor Social Security payments of all workers. NIPA statistics measure these concepts but only at two-digit level. By applying C_t to the compensation of total labor of each four-digit industries we are assuming that, within each two-digit sector, all industries pay the same proportion of wages to those working in the administrative units, and that Social Security payments are also the same proportion for each sector. When calculating in Chapter 4 the four inputs-based SR, the application of the same coefficient C_t to both the compensation of production workers and that of non-production workers has two implications. First, we are assuming that the proportionality across four-digit industries is maintained for both production and non-production workers; and second, we are over-adjusting the share of production workers, since the adjusting factor C_t takes into account the undermeasurement of the wages of workers in auxiliary units in our panel, and these workers should be considered as only non-production workers. This over-adjustment has a parallel in an under-adjustment of non-production workers.

However, these problems do not seem to affect significantly our results. As we will see in Chapters 4 and 5, the VAR models we apply to the three-inputs SR and to the four-inputs SR yield similar results.

In Table 2.2 we present the input shares avegared over time and over four-digit industries for each two-digit sector, and their standard errors. The first column gives the share of total labor compensation as calculated directly with out data set, without any adjustments. The second column includes the same data after the adjustment, whereas column 3 presents the share of intermediate inputs.

The pattern of shares among sectors is quite homogeneous. Pre-adjusted labor shares account on average 24% of nominal output. This figure is increased to 30.8% on average after we adjust, with a maximum of 41.2% in sector 38 Instruments and a minimum in 21 Tobacco, with 16.9%. The distribution between production and non-production workers (not presented in the table) is 2/3 and 1/3, respectively, although in practice these shares should be slightly closer to each other if we take into account the under-adjustment for non-production workers. Finally, the share of materials is on average of 49.7%. This distribution of inputs compensation is quite stable, as we can detect by observing their relatively small standard errors. However, if we look at the tendency of shares given in Table 2.3, we can observe that there is a slight downward tendency in the labor share for most sectors, and a positive tendency for materials.

In the table we present the results of regressing the shares on time. We have calculated the trend of each share for every four-digit industry, and averaged them over two-digit sectors. The standard error is the square root of an unweighted average of the variances at four-digit level. Both the trend coefficient and the standard error are multiplied by 100 in the table, to avoid very small numbers. The negative slope of labor share is due to the share of production workers. However, this coefficients, which are clearly significant, are not of a very large magnitude. The largest coefficient we find for production workers is -0.00316, for sector 38 Instruments. This means that over the 26 years of the sample period the share has decreased on average in 8.2 percentage points, for an average share of 20%. For the remaining sectors the tendency is much lower, as it is also the case for the adjusted share of total workers: an average tendency of -0.0015 implies a total change of 3.3% in the whole period. The shares of intermediate inputs are not stable either, although the pattern of change is very diverse among sectors. For some of them the share has increased, whereas for others it has remained stable or decreased. Overall, we can conclude that input shares have not been the same during the 26 years of the sample period (something which would have been a real surprise for such a large sample and such a large number of industries), but that the change has not been very large.

NOTES

[1]This amount would be considerably reduced if we included Food Products, since these are non-durables and are grouped in 47 four-digit subsectors.

[2]We only use the data until 1984, since we adjust the labor share with NIPA data, which covers only until that year. The adjustment is described below.

[3]The present documentation is taken from Gray (1989).

[4]See, for example, Martin (1993), p.432.

[5]See the comments about value-added data in the introductory chapter. In all of these articles, the use of intermediate inputs would have reduced considerably the high estimates of markups and returns to scale.

[6]As mentioned in the introduction, a further bias arises from the inappropriate method for calculating value added for some manufacturing industries in the Bureau of Economic Analysis (the source of the data used by Hall), as shown by Waldmann (1991).

[7]The most careful analyses of the flaws of value-added data when there is no competition are Basu and Fernald (1994) and (1995), already cited, in which they re-assess the work by Hall (1990) on increasing returns to scale and the work by Caballero and Lyons (1992) on externalities.

[8]He refers to the data used in Dommowitz et al. (1988), which was developed from the same sources as ours.

[9]Unfortunately, we do not have information on materials cost from the NIPA to correct the shares of our intermediate inputs.

[10]The reason for doing this is that in Chapters 3 and 5 we compare results obtained with the Solow residual and the Dual Solow residual, and we cannot construct DSRs with two different types of labor prices. For coherence between the SR and the DSR equations we use the same number of inputs.

Appendix 1: Tables

Table 2.1: *Number of sub-sectors, sum of value added and average of total value added for each two-digit sector.*

Sector	Sub-Sectors	VA	% VA
21 Tobacco	4	5867	1%
22 Textile Mill	30	24289	4%
23 Apparel	33	26527	4%
24 Lumber-Wood	17	19962	3%
25 Furniture	13	9992	2%
26 Paper	17	27153	4%
27 Printing	16	30232	5%
28 Chemicals	28	53289	8%
29 Petroleum-Coal	5	27355	4%
30 Rubber-Plastic	6	18339	3%
31 Leather	11	5680	1%
32 Stone-Glass	27	19701	3%
33 Primary Metals	26	54364	8%
34 Fabr. Metals	36	47965	7%
35 Machinery	44	102521	16%
36 Electric Machinery	39	56363	9%
37 Transp. Equipment	17	92725	14%
38 Instruments	13	16791	3%
39 Miscellaneous	20	10525	2%

Note: 'VA' is value added in million dollars and it is an average over the sample period (1958-84) of the summation over four-digit sectors. '% VA' is the percentage on total value added for the 19 manufacturing sectors considered here (that is, excluding 20 Food Products).

Table 2.2: *Average input shares: Unweighted average (over four-digit sectors) of means (over time) and square root of the average of the variance.*

	α		α_{adj}		β	
SIC	Share	s.e.	Share	s.e.	Share	s.e.
21	0.111	0.016	0.169	0.027	0.555	0.044
22	0.217	0.027	0.267	0.033	0.581	0.042
23	0.252	0.026	0.298	0.030	0.523	0.042
24	0.228	0.030	0.295	0.033	0.573	0.037
25	0.277	0.025	0.337	0.027	0.475	0.024
26	0.212	0.025	0.272	0.023	0.535	0.041
27	0.346	0.044	0.391	0.042	0.331	0.031
28	0.150	0.028	0.220	0.032	0.501	0.062
29	0.102	0.022	0.194	0.027	0.678	0.048
30	0.263	0.026	0.341	0.029	0.468	0.033
31	0.269	0.030	0.346	0.027	0.500	0.029
32	0.285	0.035	0.368	0.028	0.406	0.038
33	0.206	0.031	0.267	0.031	0.594	0.050
34	0.265	0.030	0.326	0.031	0.478	0.034
35	0.289	0.032	0.359	0.029	0.429	0.034
36	0.267	0.037	0.342	0.043	0.438	0.041
37	0.268	0.037	0.342	0.039	0.524	0.042
38	0.306	0.034	0.412	0.039	0.364	0.031
39	0.251	0.031	0.309	0.032	0.468	0.031

Note: α is the share of labor before the adjustments, whereas α_{adj} is after adjustment. β is the share of intermediate inputs. The expression 's.e.' stands for standard error.

Table 2.3: *Unweighted average trend of input shares: slope of regression on time and its standard error.*

	α		α_{adj}		β	
SIC	Share	s.e.	Share	s.e.	Share	s.e.
21	-0.035	0.022	0.091	0.035	-0.390	0.069
22	-0.082	0.056	0.058	0.070	-0.073	0.088
23	-0.107	0.052	0.096	0.063	-0.252	0.077
24	-0.271	0.041	-0.184	0.060	0.130	0.072
25	-0.233	0.041	-0.147	0.062	0.016	0.052
26	-0.233	0.041	-0.072	0.052	0.164	0.085
27	-0.418	0.064	-0.063	0.099	-0.036	0.051
28	-0.252	0.047	-0.158	0.067	0.399	0.097
29	-0.253	0.027	-0.252	0.046	0.328	0.108
30	-0.248	0.045	-0.189	0.065	0.081	0.078
31	-0.305	0.042	-0.116	0.059	0.018	0.066
32	-0.349	0.044	-0.078	0.060	0.252	0.066
33	-0.247	0.047	-0.084	0.063	0.270	0.095
34	-0.258	0.051	-0.183	0.062	-0.010	0.070
35	-0.300	0.050	-0.127	0.061	0.143	0.065
36	-0.267	0.063	-0.178	0.085	0.077	0.083
37	-0.296	0.056	0.068	0.082	-0.096	0.081
38	-0.323	0.049	-0.216	0.073	0.030	0.057
39	-0.308	0.047	-0.233	0.061	0.088	0.069

Note: The trend is calculated for each four-digit sector and averaged within each two-digit sector. α is the share of labor before the adjustments, whereas α_{adj} is after adjustment. β is the share of intermediate inputs. The numbers presented are 100 times larger than the actual numbers. This has been done in order to avoid very small figures.

3

Estimating Markups Using Productivity Measures

This chapter deals with the estimation of markups in manufacturing sectors of the US, using Hall's non-parametric approach of the SR equation and extending it to its dual version, the DSR equation. We benefit from the information of a very large data panel and from two equations that involve very different type of variables (quantities and prices).

The estimation of price-cost margins through the implicit correlation of the SR and instruments of demand is just a replication of Hall's (1988) results. We use gross output data instead of value added, and data on four-digit SIC industries (pooling them to obtain markups for two-digit industries, thus concentrating the information). The correction of the labor share with NIPA figures, as described in the previous chapter, is an improvement to Domowitz et al. (1988) paper. But the main point we make in this chapter is that the DSR can be different from zero in the presence of materials price shocks, and that the correlation of the DSR with the increase in materials prices can be used for calculating markups. Although Shapiro (1987) and Roeger (1995) have argued that the DSR reflects mainly technology, we will see that this is not necessarily true: demand shocks and oil shocks may affect both the SR and the DSR, and may therefore explain the correlation between them, since demand and oil shocks happen to be highly correlated for most of our sample period.

The main empirical results of our study are two. First, we obtain statistically significant and high estimates of price-cost margins for most two-digit SIC industries. These results confirm those obtained by Hall (1988), Domowitz et al. (1988) and Roeger (1995). Second, our results with the SR equation and the DSR are very close to each other, adding to the robustness of our estimates. These two facts give new evidence of Hall's original conjecture, i.e. the cyclical movement of the SR is explained by the existence of markups.

The chapter is organized as follows. Section 3.1 presents the derivation of the SR and the DSR when there exist markups and non-constant returns to scale, and examines how they are affected by alternative shocks. It is worth noting in advance an important point about notation in order to avoid confusions. As we will see, the only real "measures" of productivity growth are the SR and the DSR calculated under competition and constant returns to scale, because in this case the elasticities are equal to revenue shares. Dropping these assumptions is useful for deriving an estimating equation, but it means that true productivity growth is no longer observable. We will use starred names for the unobservable expressions of true productivity change and non-starred names for the measures under the standard assumptions. Section 3.2 discusses the econometric techniques chosen to pool the data. Section 3.3 introduces the instrumental variables used for the estimation. The results of the chapter are presented in the remaining 3 sections. First we provide the estimated markups using sectoral instrumental variables, and discuss the preliminary regressions we run before arriving to our definitive estimates (once we adopt the assumption of constant returns to scale and we reduce the number of sectoral instrumental variables). Then we test for the overidentifying restrictions of standard aggregate instruments (oil prices, import prices, defence expenditures) and show that they are not adequate instruments. Finally, we provide the results of the exogeneity test (using Hall's expression) of the SR and the DSR, and the one of both residuals once the inputs' shares have been corrected for the markup. We will see that the *corrected* residuals are not significantly correlated with GNP growth or oil prices, suggesting that they are better measures of productivity growth.

3.1 Estimating Equations

3.1.1 Solow Residual

Consider the following production function faced by the representative firm at each period t:

$$Y_t = A_t F_t(N_t, M_t, K_t) = A_t X_t$$

where Y_t is production, A_t is an index of Hick's-neutral technology and $X_t = F(N_t, M_t, K_t)$ is a constant, homogeneous of degree γ function of N_t, the labor input, M_t, intermediate inputs, and K_t, capital, all measured at time t. We can differenciate the logarithm of the production function and obtain an expression for the growth rate of output as a function of the growth rate of technology change and the growth rate of inputs,

$$\frac{\Delta Y_t}{Y_t} = \frac{\Delta A_t}{A_t} + \varepsilon_{Nt}\frac{\Delta N_t}{N_t} + \varepsilon_{Mt}\frac{\Delta M_t}{M_t} + \varepsilon_{Kt}\frac{\Delta K_t}{K_t}$$

where ε_{Nt}, ε_{Mt}, and ε_{Kt} are, respectively, the elasticities of F with respect to N_t, M_t and K_t:

$$\begin{aligned} \varepsilon_{Nt} &= F_{Nt}\frac{N_t}{X_t} \\ \varepsilon_{Mt} &= F_{Mt}\frac{M_t}{X_t} \\ \varepsilon_{Kt} &= F_{Kt}\frac{K_t}{X_t} \end{aligned}$$

and F_{Nt}, F_{Mt}, F_{Kt} are the marginal productivities of these factors. From here we can calculate technology change, which is unobservable, as the difference between output growth and weighted inputs. We will use lower case letters to express log differences of the variables. We will also omit time subscripts.

$$a = y - (\varepsilon_N\ n + \varepsilon_M\ m + \varepsilon_K\ k) \tag{3.1}$$

$$a = y - x$$

Here a is true technological progress. As explained above, we will use $SR^* \equiv a$ to refer to true technological progress and SR

(the traditional measure) to refer to estimates of SR^* under the standard assumptions of perfect competition and constant returns to scale.

Static profit maximization under imperfect competition implies

$$F_N = \frac{W}{MC} = \mu \frac{W}{P}$$
$$F_M = \frac{V}{MC} = \mu \frac{V}{P}$$
$$F_K = \frac{R}{MC} = \mu \frac{R}{P}$$

where μ is the ratio of price (P) to marginal cost (MC), and W, V and R are the prices of labor, materials and capital services, respectively. This allows us to write elasticities in terms of factors' revenue shares S_N, S_M, S_K and the markup,

$$\varepsilon_N = F_N \frac{N}{X} = \mu S_N$$
$$\varepsilon_M = F_M \frac{M}{X} = \mu S_M$$
$$\varepsilon_K = F_K \frac{K}{X} = \mu S_K$$

Euler's theorem for homogeneous functions implies

$$X = \frac{1}{\gamma} (F_N N + F_M M + F_K K)$$

which gives in turn the sum of the elasticities of F as equal to the degree of homogeneity, that is, equal to γ. Given the last two sets of equations we can then rewrite (3.1) as follows:

$$SR^* \equiv a = y - \mu S_N n - \mu S_M m - \mu S_K k;$$

or

$$SR^* = y - \mu S_N n - \mu S_M m - (\gamma - \mu S_N - \mu S_M) k$$

Solow (1957) assumed constant returns to scale and competition to measure productivity growth in the long run. Under these assumptions, non observable μ and γ disappear, and technology changes become

$$SR^* = SR = (y - k) - S_N (n - k) - S_M (m - k)$$

The SR is thus the "residual" of the growth rate of the output-capital ratio once we account for the growth rate of weighted labor-capital and materials-capital ratios, the weights being their respective revenue shares. We can express true productivity change SR^* as the sum of the Solow residual SR plus a bias that depends on the parameters of scale γ, the markup μ and weighted inputs' growth,

$$SR^* = SR - (\mu - 1)\ [S_N\ (n-k) + S_M\ (m-k)] - (\gamma - 1)\ k \quad (3.2)$$

Recall that all variables have an (omitted) time subscript, since all the equations arise from year on year optimization problems.

3.1.2 Dual Solow Residual

Shapiro (1987) derives the dual expression of productivity change under Solow's original assumptions.[1] It can be extended to the case of markups and non-constant returns to scale. As before, we consider a homogeneous of degree γ production function where factors are paid in proportion to their marginal product and firms set prices at a markup on their marginal cost. Costs in this case will be equal to

$$C = (\frac{Y}{A})^{\frac{1}{\gamma}}\ g(W, V, R)$$

Here $g(W, V, R)$ depends only on factor prices. Homogeneity is the reason for the separability of $\frac{Y}{A}$ and γ from prices. Marginal cost will be

$$\begin{aligned} MC &= \frac{1}{\gamma Y}\ (\frac{Y}{A})^{\frac{1}{\gamma}}\ g(W, V, R) \\ &= \frac{C}{\gamma\, Y} \quad (3.3) \\ &= \frac{AC}{\gamma} \end{aligned}$$

where AC is average cost. Since we have ruled out any fixed costs in the production function, the ratio of average cost to marginal cost becomes an indicator of returns to scale.

In order to obtain the DSR, we difference the logarithm of the marginal cost equation (3.3). Because we have assumed a constant function F, the degree of returns to scale will also be fixed. We will also assume that markups are constant.[2] Log-differentiation yields

$$mc = (\frac{1}{\gamma} - 1)\, y + \frac{g_W(.)}{g(.)}\, dW + \frac{g_V(.)}{g(.)}\, dV + \frac{g_R(.)}{g(.)}\, dR - \frac{1}{\gamma}\, a \quad (3.4)$$

where $g_W(.)$, $g_V(.)$ and $g_R(.)$ are the derivatives of the function $g(.)$ and mc is the growth rate of marginal cost. Using Shephard's lemma we can derive conditional factor demands from the cost function:

$$\begin{aligned} N &= \frac{\partial C}{\partial W} = (\frac{Y}{A})^{(\frac{1}{\gamma})}\, g_W \\ M &= \frac{\partial C}{\partial V} = (\frac{Y}{A})^{(\frac{1}{\gamma})}\, g_V \\ K &= \frac{\partial C}{\partial R} = (\frac{Y}{A})^{(\frac{1}{\gamma})}\, g_R \end{aligned}$$

which implies that

$$\begin{aligned} \frac{g_W}{g} &= \frac{N}{(\frac{Y}{A})^{(\frac{1}{\gamma})}\, g(.)} = \frac{N}{C} \\ \frac{g_V}{g} &= \frac{M}{(\frac{Y}{A})^{(\frac{1}{\gamma})}\, g(.)} = \frac{M}{C} \\ \frac{g_K}{g} &= \frac{K}{(\frac{Y}{A})^{(\frac{1}{\gamma})}\, g(.)} = \frac{K}{C} \end{aligned} \quad (3.5)$$

By substituting the expressions in (3.5) into (3.4) we obtain productivity growth as

$$a = (1-\gamma)\, y + \gamma\, (\frac{NW}{C})\, w + \gamma\, (\frac{MV}{C})\, v + \gamma\, (\frac{KR}{C})\, r - \gamma\, mc$$

If markups are fixed, the growth rate of the output price is equal to the growth rate of marginal cost. Furthermore, the relationship between AC and MC in (3.3) and markup pricing give us the equivalence between cost shares and revenue shares. For each factor z:

$$\gamma\, C_Z = \mu\, S_Z$$

where C_Z refers to the cost share of input Z. We use these equivalences and Euler theorem to obtain a measure of productivity change based on revenue shares:

$$a = (1-\gamma)\, y + \mu\, S_N\, (w-p) + \mu\, S_M\, (v-p) + \mu\, S_K\, (r-p) \quad (3.6)$$

Shapiro calculates a particular case of this measure directly using value-added data: one with no markups under the assumption of constant returns to scale, i.e. with μ and γ equal to one. This is the dual version of the Solow measure, under Solow's assumptions. Shapiro also argues that the assumption of perfect adjustment of capital is clearly wrong, so he derives his measure relaxing the flexibility of capital and assuming that the quantity of capital is fixed in the short run. To calculate the optimality conditions in this adjustment costs version the production function has to be parametrized. Shapiro uses the Constant Elasticity of Substitution function and the Cobb-Douglas function with constant returns to scale. His results do not vary much under these two different specifications, so here we retain for simplicity the Cobb-Douglas function, also supported by the evidence given in Chapter 2 that factor shares (which, in the absence of markups, reflect the elasticities of the production function) have a very small variability and have changed little over time. The Cobb-Douglas assumption implies that the growth rate of the real rental price of capital, $r - p$, is approximated by the growth rate of output per unit of capital, $y - k$, when capital is fixed in the short run. Under these conditions the Shapiro dual residual becomes

$$DSR = S_N\ (w - p) + S_M\ (v - p) + (1 - S_K - S_M)\ (y - k)$$

This approach has the advantage of avoiding the use of the rental price of capital, which has well known measurement problems.

The adjustment costs version of the DSR in equation (3.6), in the case of a Cobb-Douglas technology with non-constant returns to scale and imperfect competition is derived in Appendix 1 at the end of the chapter, and yields the following expression

$$\begin{aligned} DSR^* \quad = \quad & \mu\ S_N\ (w - p) + \mu\ S_M\ (v - p) + \\ & + (1 - \mu\ S_K - \mu\ S_M)\ (y - k) + (\gamma - 1)\ k \end{aligned} \tag{3.7}$$

We denote this measure DSR* to distinguish it from Shapiro's DSR. Analogous to what we did in Section 3.1.1 for the SR, we can express this true productivity growth DSR* as the sum of the DSR and a function of the inputs' prices, which can be seen as the bias in the DSR due to not allowing for imperfect competition and scale economies,

$$DSR^* = DSR + (\gamma - 1)k + (\mu - 1)\,[S_N(w-p) + +S_M(v-p) + (S_N + S_M)(y-k)] \quad (3.8)$$

3.1.3 Estimation of Markups

Let us rewrite equations (3.2) and (3.8) in the following way:

$$SR = (\mu - 1)\,[S_N\,(n-k) + S_M\,(m-k)] + (\gamma - 1)\,k + SR* \quad (3.9)$$

$$DSR = -(\mu - 1)\,[S_N(w-p) + S_M(v-p) + +(S_N + S_M)(y-k)] - (\gamma - 1)k + DSR^* \quad (3.10)$$

In the absence of measurement errors in variables, and assuming perfectly competitive inputs' markets and constant markups, the SR* and the DSR* are the correct expressions of true productivity change. They should therefore be equal to each other, because they are alternative measures of the same thing. Also, provided there is no contemporaneous influence of demand on productivity, they should be uncorrelated with good instruments of demand, because both of them measure shifts in the production function.

These two issues are used by Hall and Shapiro in deriving their tests for competition and constant returns to scale. If these two assumptions are true, then the SR* and the DSR* equal the original SR and DSR, as it is clear from the preceding equations. In this case, the SR (and the DSR) should also be uncorrelated with demand (as argued by Hall) and the SR should be close to the DSR (as argued by Shapiro).

Considering the first issue, namely the lack of correlation of productivity measures with demand, one can look at the exogeneity of the SR and the DSR as a test of the plausibility of the assumptions under which they are constructed. If they are correlated with an instrument which is assumed to be exogenous to productivity change, i.e. orthogonal to SR* and DSR*, it must be because they are correlated with the first two terms on the right hand side of their respective equations (3.9 and 3.10). In this case, either markups or the degree of returns to scale (or possibly both) are different from one.

Hall's value-added data reject the hypothesis of exogenous SR for most one-digit and two-digit sectors. Having rejected the null hypothesis, he uses the value-added version of equation (3.9) to estimate markups under the assumption of constant returns and obtains very high values ($\frac{\mu}{1-S_M}$=2 for durables and $\frac{\mu}{1-S_M}$=3 for non-durables; the denominator corrects for the fact that he uses value-added data). These results are confirmed by the analysis of Dommowitz et al. (1988) using a gross output function and a more disaggregated data set (very similar to the one used here), although the point estimates they obtain are much lower (and plausible) than those of Hall.

Shapiro tests the hypothesis of no demand shocks by looking at the second issue noted above, namely the correlation of the SR with the DSR. He runs the following regression:

$$SR = a + b\,DSR + u \tag{3.11}$$

If productivity shocks are important and the SR measures true shifts in the production function, as it is claimed by RBC theories, then the coefficient b should be identically equal to one. If the SR includes some demand component, as argued in traditional labor hoarding theories and in the markups/increasing returns hypothesis, then the DSR should not move with the cycle (because factor prices would remain unchanged), and b should be different from one and possibly insignificant. Shapiro finds that he cannot reject the null hypothesis of $b = 1$, and that adding a demand variable to (3.11) (in his case, GNP growth) does not help in explaining the SR.

However, it is not necessarily true that the Keynesian alternative, as Shapiro calls it, cannot explain the observed correlation between the SR and the DSR. In particular, it could be the case that changes in demand and the existence of markups (possibly combined with labor hoarding, or increasing returns to scale) explain the cyclical behavior the SR, whereas materials price shocks and markups explain the DSR. Looking at equation (3.10) it is apparent that an increase in materials prices will cause a negative DSR.[3] The idea behind the use of the DSR as a measure of productivity change is that factor prices, which reflect their marginal productivity, move only with technology shocks. In particular, and this is a key point in Shapiro's argument, changes in demand will not change input prices. However, oil shocks are not technology shocks (the production function is not altered by a change in energy prices) but they induce a change in the price of intermediate inputs that is reflected in the DSR if there are markups. At the same time, oil shocks produce an obvious change in aggregate demand that can induce a bias in the SR. Therefore, a positive correlation between the SR and the DSR may be the result of a combination of synchronized oil shocks, demand shocks and markups.

To sum up, the observed high correlation between the SR and the DSR may reflect changes in the technology of a competitive economy, but the alternative explanation of margins/increasing returns cannot be ruled out. Therefore, using appropriate instruments, we can use both measures of productivity to calculate markups and returns to scale, in the same way as Hall does for the SR equation. If we treat the productivity change as a series of independently distributed shocks orthogonal to demand (i.e., ruling out aggregate shocks to technology), the SR* and the DSR* can be treated as the disturbance term in the estimating equations. By introducing a dummy variable for each sector, we are assuming therefore that true technology changes are white noise plus a constant (the same assumption that Hall uses for estimating consistently the markup). This constant gives us, for every sector, the growth rate of technology. The SR and the DSR will not be random,[4] because they co-vary with the right-hand side of the equations. It is exactly this failure of the exogeneity of the SR and the DSR the basis that make us say that they are not measures of pure productivity changes.

We can estimate both equations separately and compare the markups obtained. If specification and measurement errors of the variables are small, both should give similar results, since our model implies that constant markups and increasing returns are the only factors that bias the SR and the DSR in measuring true productivity. Then we can estimate both equations jointly as a system and restrict the key parameters to be equal, thus gaining efficiency in the estimation.

Our preliminary estimating equations are therefore expressions (3.9) and (3.10). Since the estimation of the parameter of returns to scale is very inefficient, we prefer to drop it and estimate the same equations restricting γ to be one in the second stage. This amounts to assuming constant returns to scale and to allowing for markups, a combination which does not seem to be compatible with the absence of substantial profit rates in US manufacturing industries. We do not believe that the assumption of constant returns to scale is necessarily true. Increasing returns are no doubt important and necessary in explaining the high markups we obtain, so that omitting capital from the equation can bias the results.[5] But, on the other hand, our data on capital is not informative enough to give the degree of returns to scale, as will be apparent from the results of the preliminary regressions. Furthermore, the difference in the markups estimated with and without capital (that is, with γ not estimated and set to one) is small for most sectors, so presumably the bias for omitting the variable is also small. It should be clear however that we do not rule out the possibility of increasing returns, and we believe it is one of the main alternatives for explaining the high level of markups.

As mentioned in the introduction, Roeger (1995) independently uses the same model as we do here to estimate the markup, although his assumptions and interpretation of the sources of fluctuations is entirely different from ours. He shows that the difference between the SR and the DSR (calculated with the rental price of capital r, i.e. assuming that r reflects correctly the marginal productivity of capital) is equal to an expression which has the markup as a parameter. More precisely, he recovers μ from the equation

$$SR - DSR = B\ [(y-k) + (p-r)] + u \qquad (3.12)$$

Here B is the Lerner index $(\frac{P-MC}{P})$, which is a transformation of our μ. The main advantage of this estimating equation is that we do not need to rely on instrumental variables, because the disturbance term does not depend on true technology change, as in each of the individual equations. This procedure is analogous to pooling the SR and the DSR equations as it is done in our model. However, in Roeger's interpretation all the variables in the model are driven by technology. The original measures of productivity have to be corrected by the estimated markups; once this is done, they reflect technology changes.

The argument he uses to rule out the possibility of demand shocks is in our opinion not valid. He tests the demand alternative by adding real GNP changes to equation (3.12) to investigate the possibility of labor hoarding or excess capacity, and obtains a low and insignificant coefficient for GNP. But this is not a correct way to test for demand shocks, since, once sectoral output is introduced in the equation (which probably reflects demand), it is not clear why an aggregate instrument would add explanatory power to the regression. At lower levels of aggregation any sectoral variable will be more correlated with the sectoral SR or DSR than any aggregate instrument, so that it is not surprising that adding aggregate GNP growth to the equation will not yield any significant coefficient. Sectoral output growth in his model picks up all the correlation; adding an aggregate instrument on top of it and interpreting it as the only demand influence amounts to assuming *a priori* that sectoral output growth is driven by technology. The use of instrumental variables in estimating his equation would be a more natural test of the influence of demand, since it allows for the possibility of demand driven fluctuations in the regressors.

3.2 Econometric Method

We estimate each equation for all two-digit SIC sectors by pooling four-digit industries within each of them, and using standard fixed-effects. That is, each two-digit industry is treated as a system of four-digit sub-sectors with a common slope (the parameters that give us μ and γ) and a different intercept for each sub-sector, allowing for time-invariant differences among them. The fixed effects assumption implies that productivity growth in each sub-sector may have different trend whereas the common slope indicates that constant markups are equal within each two-digit industry. In this way we allow for different growth rates of measured productivity for each four-digit industry.

The disturbances in our model represent true technological shocks whereas average growth in technology is given by the dummy variable. This affects the estimation in two respects. First, there is a problem of endogeneity because of the likely correlation of the residual with the regressors (weighted inputs) which requires the utilization of an instrumental variables estimator. Second, it is possible that the disturbances of different sub-sectors are contemporaneously correlated because of common technology shocks (at least within two-digit sectors). These two problems would point to the use of a 3SLS estimator. However, in a first stage we use a 2SLS estimator with standard errors derived from a variance-covariance matrix of the estimated coefficients that is consistent if disturbances are heteroskedastic and correlated across four-digit sub-sectors in the same two-digit industry (with different correlation of different pairs of four-digit groups). The correlation between groups can also vary with time. We will use hencefore the expression "heteroskedasticity-robust standard errors" to refer to this type of variance-covariance matrix.

The reason for the choice of 2SLS with robust standard errors rather that 3SLS estimator relies on the short time series available (26 years): a biased estimator of the covariance matrix of the residuals in the second step of 3SLS can lead to a substantial bias in the final estimation of the coefficients. We choose 2SLS which is efficient only if there is a common variance of the disturbances for all periods and sub-sectors (within two-digit sectors) and no cross-correlation between them. Since this will probably not be the case, we correct the standard errors of the estimators to make them consistent against both contemporaneous cross-correlation and within- and across-sectors heteroskedasticity.

Once we estimate our equations with heteroskedasticity-robust standard errors for the coefficients, we apply some tests for the autocorrelation of the residuals. These tests do not provide a uniform conclusion over all industries' residuals, so we re-run our regressions and calculate standard errors for the coefficients that are robust not only to heteroskedasticity, but also to autocorrelation. We will see that the efficiency of the estimates hardly changes with the new standard errors.

The specification of the model for each two-digit sector is therefore

$$Y_{it} = \alpha_i + \beta X_{it} + v_{it} \qquad v_{it} \sim N(0, \sigma^2) \tag{3.13}$$

where Y_{it} is the SR or the DSR of the four-digit sector i at time t, X_{ti} is the corresponding vector of regressors and v_{it} is the residual.

The 2SLS estimator is

$$\hat{\beta} = (X'PX)^{-1}X'PY$$

where X and Y are the stacked matrices of the regressors (including the dummies that allow for fixed effects) and the dependent variable and

$$P = I_N \otimes W(W'W)^{-1}W'$$

Here W (of size $T \times k$) is the matrix of k instruments. The heteroskedasticity-consistent variance matrix of β is given by

$$var(\hat{\beta}) = (X'PX)^{-1}S(X'PX)^{-1} \tag{3.14}$$

where S is the matrix

$$S = \sum_{i=1}^{N}\sum_{j=1}^{N}\sum_{t=1}^{T} \tilde{X}_t^{i\prime}\tilde{X}_t^{j} e_{it}e_{jt}$$

The variables e_{it} and e_{jt} correspond to the residuals of the individual instrumental variables estimation of equation (3.13) for sectors i and j, and N and T are the number of sectors and time periods, respectively. $\tilde{X}_t^i$ and $\tilde{X}_t^j$ refer to the instrumented regressors that result from the first stage of the 2SLS estimator, i.e. the projections of the regressors of industries i and j on instruments W (which are common for all groups within two-digit industries):

$$\tilde{X}_t^i = X_t^{i\prime}W(W'W)^{-1}W'$$

The expression of the variance-covariance matrix for β when we want to make it robust to heteroskedasticity *and* autocorrelation is similar to the one in equation 3.14, but in this case matrix S becomes

$$S = \sum_{k=-p}^{k=p}\sum_{i=1}^{N}\sum_{j=1}^{N}\sum_{t=1}^{T} \tilde{X}_{t+k}^{i\prime}\tilde{X}_t^{j} e_{it+k}e_{jt} \tag{3.15}$$

where p is the order of autocorrelation of the residuals against which the new covariance matrix is robust. The new formula for S implies that we are summing $2 \times p \times T \times N^2$ more elements than in the previous expression (3.2).

3.3 Instruments

Much has been written about the availability of good aggregate instruments for demand. The ones used by Hall were originally proposed by Ramey (1991), and they have been used extensively in the literature.[6] These aggregate instruments have been heavily criticized for their lack of power and for their possible endogeneity. In particular, the fact that in Hall's investigation the only instrument that works well is the oil price casts some doubt on the validity of his results. Hall replies to these criticisms responding that a good instrument must not shift the production function, and that oil prices clearly do not shift the production function in the annual horizon considered in his investigation.[7]

In our case, both oil prices and import prices could be especially suitable because they reflect demand shocks as well as materials price shocks, and hence are as powerful for the DSR as for the SR. However, as it will be shown in Section 3.5, the use of several aggregate instruments imposes false overidentifying restrictions on the model, and can therefore bias the results. It is also the case that when using each instrument separately we obtain strikingly different results from the case in which they are used jointly.

In this paper we prefer to take as benchmark estimates those calculated with sectoral instrumental variables, as suggested by Jimeno (1989). For each two-digit sector equation, the instruments used are the SRs (for the SR equation) and the DSRs (for the DSR equation) of those other sectors that are not related with it through input-output linkages. The residuals used as instruments are aggregated from four-digit to two-digit sectors. The list of sectoral instruments for each industry is taken from Jimeno's paper, although after running the first regressions, we test for the lack of overidentifying restrictions imposed by the instruments (as described in the following section), and start a selection of a suitable list of intruments for each sector. Although the best option would be to use, for each two-digit sectors, only those instruments that pass the test in both the SR and the DSR equations, following this criteria would make us count on very few sectors in some cases. For that reason, we will introduce some flexibility in the final selection of instrumental variables, as we will explain later.

The list of instrumental variables originally proposed by Jimeno can be found in Appendix 2.

3.4 Results

3.4.1 *Estimation of markups and returns to scale.*

All our results are provided in Appendix 3. Table 3.3 presents the results of estimating equations (3.9) and (3.10) without restricting the parameter γ that corresponds to the degree of returns to scale. Markups in all tables are tranformed into price-cost margins (PCM), defined as

$$PCM = \frac{P - MC}{P}$$

where P is the output price and MC is marginal cost.

As stressed in Section 3.1.3, the estimation of the coefficient for capital is very inaccurate and varies a lot for different sectors, giving in many cases results without economic sense. The high standard errors and the corresponding imprecision of the estimated γ values in the table are results which are typical for analyses that use sectoral data to estimate production functions directly with inputs on the right hand side of the equation. Our estimating equations can be seen as a transformation of a production function, and they incorporate all the problems associated with capital measurement.[8]

Estimated values for γ are within a very large range around one. For some sectors it is even negative (31 Leather, 32 Stone and Glass, 38 Instruments in the SR equation; 21 Tobacco, 29 Petroleum and Coal, 31 Leather products and 38 Instruments in the DSR equation), for other sectors it is greater than 2 (26 Paper, 33 Primary Metals for SR; 26 Paper, 28 Chemicals, 33 Primary Metals, 34 Fabricated Metals for DSR). Only in a couple of sectors there is a "reasonable" value close to 1 or slightly larger, with small standard errors.

In Table 3.4 there is a comparison between the averages and the standard deviations of the growth rates of the three inputs considered, i.e. labor, materials and capital. The numbers are unweighted averages over time and over four-digit industries, the figures for the standard deviations being square roots of averaged variances. It can be appreciated how the standard deviations for capital growth are normally less than half of those of materials growth or labor growth. This low variability may explain the poor results of the coefficient linked to capital. On average the standard deviation of capital growth is 0.07 (and this value is upwardly influenced by sectors 22 and 23), whereas the figure for labor growth is 0.11 and that for materials 0.15. A more disaggregated examination of these variables (standard errors over time for each four-digit industry) would show an ever greater difference between the variability of capital and the other inputs.

In what follows we supress capital as an independent regressor; therefore it is implicitly assumed a constant returns to scale technology. Even if this assumption is incorrect and a certain degree of returns to scale compensates the profitability derived from margins, the bias in the estimation is presumably low. Furthermore, our results under constant returns are directly comparable with those of Hall and his critics.

3.4.2 Estimation of Margins Under Constant Returns to Scale.

Selection of the Set of Instruments.

In this section we look and the selection process of the adequate instruments for the 2SLS estimation, using the criterion of a test for overidentification restrictions. The process will not be completely satisfactory, since the number of instruments is reduced to one in some cases, and we arrive at a point in which we may rely only on one sector as a valid instrument. Estimates may turn out to be very poor. At the end of the process we will conclude that for some sectors an OLS estimator is more adequate than 2SLS.

Table 3.5 reports the estimation of the PCM under the assumption of constant returns to scale using the original sectoral instrumental variables, i.e. those sectors suggested by Jimeno (1989) in his paper. The variables used as instruments are the SRs and DSRs of non-related sectors.[9] We do not take the estimates of Table 3.5 as definitive, since the margins for some industries have been calculated with invalid instrumental variables, as the overidentification tests reveal.

The t-values of the overidentification test can be found in Tables 3.6 and 3.7, which correspond, respectively, to the SR and the DSR equations. The test involves looking at the significance level of each one of the instrumental variables when added as an independent regressor in the second step of 2SLS. When we find an instrument which is significant at the chosen 5% level, it means that it is redundant and is biasing the estimations of the coefficients. Therefore we reject those instruments with significant coefficients at the 5% level.

In the regressions of the test (contrary to what we do in both stages of the 2SLS estimation) we have not used fixed effects. The reason for doing this is that when there are only two instruments involved, their t-statistics will have the same absolute value (and possibly different signs). If both are significant it is not easy to decide what instrument is overidentifying the model. On the other hand, not using fixed effects in the test may yield t-values different from zero when there is only one instrument involved, and this does not make much sense from an econometric point of view, since by definition a single instrument cannot be overidentifying a model. We have used this second option and not paid much attention to the t-values of single instruments. However, if the test for overidentifying restrictions is carried out with dummy variables, the results are very similar with the ones without them.

The numbers in the second row for each industry indicate the industries which are used as instrumental variables.

A strict approach to the selection of instruments would be to reject those that are redundant for the SR *or* the DSR equations. Because the interpretation of both of them is similar, instruments should be equally valid or not valid at the same time in both cases. This is not going to be the case. For some sectors there will be instruments that are significant in one equation but not in the other. The fact that some instruments have a large t-value in the DSR equation but not in the SR equation could be rationalized by common materials price shocks: An increase in the price of oil could move all the DSRs of all sectors in the same direction, making some instruments redundant with respect of the information given by other instruments. But the opposite also happens: some instruments can have large t-values in the SR case, but not in the DSR case, and this can only be explained by a random element.

In Table 3.8 the estimation of the markup with the new instruments are presented. The results are not satisfactory for some sectors, in the sense that they provide estimates of the markup that vary a lot with respect to those with the original estimates, they give sometimes very different numbers in each equation, or they have large standard errors. The reason for this is likely to be that the remaining set of instruments used is poor. In Table 3.9, columns 2 and 5, we report the R^2 of the first stage of the 2SLS process for both equations. They are very small values, and this fact could cast some doubt on the whole estimation process. However, this low degree of correlation is found throughout this dissertation and is probably due to the fact that we are pooling together a large number of very disaggregated sectors with different behavior. We have carried out a χ^2 test for the validity of the instruments, which tells us that the instrumental variables procedure we are using is perfectly valid, since the first step of the 2SLS process gives coefficients that are highly significant (even if their R^2 is very poor).

Under the null hypothesis of zero coefficients for the instruments in the preliminary regression, the following statistic has a χ^2 distribution with as many degrees of freedom as the number of instruments involved:

$$\gamma(cov(\gamma))^{-1}\gamma$$

where γ is the vector of slopes of the first step, and the expression *cov* refers to their variance-covariance matrix.

The results of this test is given in columns 3 and 6 of Table 3.9. In the adjacent columns, we can find the degrees of freedom of the distribution (the number of instruments).

In Table 3.1 we observe that we clearly reject the null of no significance, since the 5% significance level for a χ^2 are

Table 3.1: *Significance levels of a* χ^2 *at 5% and 1%.*

Deg. freedom	5%	1%
1	3.841	6.635
2	5.991	9.210
3	7.815	11.341
4	9.488	13.277
5	11.070	15.086
6	13.388	16.812

The most interesting point is that those sectors for which bad results have been obtained with the new common instruments are those with small R^2 and small χ^2 statistics. These are industries 21 Tobacco, 23 Apparel, 28 Chemicals, 29 Petroleum, 31 Leather Products, 33 Primary Metals and 35 Machinery. All of them present a very large standard error for estimates of markups or point estimates that do not fall within a reasonable range of values.

Since restricting the number of instruments to those who pass the test in both equations at the same time does not seem to yield good results, because of the lack of enough good instruments, we look now at the estimations with a less restrictive and more pragmatic group of instrumental variables: for each equation we keep those sectors that pass the test only in that equation. The new results can be found in Table 3.10, and their overidentification tests in the following tables, 3.11 and 3.12. In Table 3.13 we have the R^2 of the first stage and the χ^2 test of the overall significance of the instruments. The results of this test have changed to more acceptable levels of markups with small standard errors for sector 33 Primary Metals and 35 Machinery. The problems with two important sectors, 28 Chemicals and 29 Petroleum, remain exactly the same as before, since the set of instruments has not changed. A similar problem affects sector 21 Tobacco and sector 31 Leather. For these industries we have calculated the markups with an OLS method, since 2SLS does not seem to work for them because of bad instruments. These results are shown in Table 3.14 (together with the ones corresponding to the rest of the industries), where it can be appreciated how the OLS results give normal levels of markups with small standard errors. We will keep the OLS estimates for these industries as our final estimations, while recognising that they may be biased.

As for the rest of the sectors, the new overidentification tests reveal that, with a few exceptions, the new sets of instruments in general do not give problems. For those industries in which we have large t-values (sectors 34 and 38 in the SR equation and 24 in the DSR equation) we have decided to leave the set of instruments as they are, since reducing it further would raise new problems of inefficient estimates. This decision may also imply a small bias in the estimation, but the alternative approach of reducing further the number of instruments or look for new combinations that give *adequate* results does not seem better, since we can fall again on the problem of inefficient estimates.

Therefore, our final estimations are those given by the sectoral instruments once a first test for overidentification has been run on the instruments, discarding those that do not pass the test in each equation independently. For sectors 21 Tobacco, 28 Chemicals, 29 Petroleum and 31 Leather we keep the OLS estimates because no group of instruments seems to yield reasonable results and because 2SLS produce inefficient estimates in at least one equation.

Testing for Autocorrelation.

Once arrived to an estimation of our equations with a final set of instruments (or OLS estimates for four sectors), we have in general a substantial degree of markups which are efficiently estimated. However, the standard errors applied up to this point are robust in front of heteroskedasticity in the residuals (and in front of contemporaneous cross-correlation among groups), but we need to analyze their possible autocorrelation pattern.

There is a very large number of series of residuals for each equation (one for every four-digit industry). Giving a summary measure of autocorrelation in a panel is necessary in order to get some information from these series. Our strategy is the following: First the Durbin-Watson (DW) statistic for each of the four-digit series in each equation is calculated in order to test for the hypothesis of no autocorrelation against the alternative of an AR(1) process. Then the t-values of an AR(2) fitted for each of these series is also presented. In order to summarize these statistics we calculate the percentage of t-values of the AR processes that pass a given significance level. Furthermore, we will fit a pooled AR(2) model to each two-digit industries' residuals with the standard dummy variables that we have been using up to now. Finally, since we get a slight indication of autocorrelation of order two, we extend the estimation with the formula of robust standard errors of the coefficients to allow for autocorrelation. The point estimates will be the same, but the new standard errors will be robust to heteroskedasticity *and* autocorrelation. As we will see, our estimates are still very efficient.

The marginal level of the DW statistic with 25 degrees of freedom and one parameter estimated is between 1.29 and 1.45 for negative autocorrelation and 2.55 and 2.71 for positive autocorrelation. Most of our 402 DW statistics (not included in the appendix) do not reject the hypothesis of no first order autocorrelation.

A second order autorrelation model (AR(2)) has also been fitted to each series of residuals. Again we have a very large amount of information, with some of the t-statistics revealing that we can reject the null of no autocorrelation at the 5% significance level. In order to obtain a summarized view of how strong is this indication of AR is, we calculate in Table 3.2 the number of t-statistics that are above some given critical levels. In the first two lines there is the percentage of two-tail t-values that are above the critical levels at 5% and 1%. These are, respectively 2.06 and 2.787 (for 26 degrees of freedom). In the following two lines the same percentage is calculated for those t-values that pass the positive (in the third line) and negative (in the fourth) one-tail critical value at 5% (1.708 and -1.708, respectively). The same is done for the 1% level in the last two lines (t-values over and under 2.485 and -2.485. The expected number of t-statistics that randomly pass their critical level should be less than 5% and 1% in the two-tail tests, and less than 2.5% and 0.5% in the one tail tests. This is not the case for any of the equations or significance levels, especially in the case of the coefficients of the second lag. Although we have to reject the null of no autocorrelation, one might argue that the evidence in favor of an AR(2) is not overwhelmingly strong. The number of high t-values is small for most series of residuals.

We apply now a method for testing autocorrelation in the residuals of a panel which should be more powerful (provided the homogeneity within two-digit sectors is large): running the AR(2) on the pooled residuals for each sector and using dummy intercepts for each sub-sector. The added power comes from a much larger number of degrees of freedom. The null hypothesis of no autocorrelation is more likely to be rejected, as it can be observed in the results. They are given in Table 3.15.

In many cases we reject the null. This result is stronger for the AR(2) coefficients than for the AR(1), and also for the DSR equation than for the SR residuals.

The comparison of the AR tests with individual four-digit series and pooling the data within two-digit is an example of the great advantage of working with disaggregated data. This is the general approach we use throughout this research, and it yields much more efficient results and a higher power for the tests than

Table 3.2: *Percentage of t-values of the first (AR1) and second (AR2) autocorrelation coefficients over the significance levels. SR and DSR equations.*

	SR-AR1	SR-AR2	DSR-AR1	DSR-AR2
5%	7.5	9.2	12.7	13.9
1%	1.5	2.5	3.0	5.0
5%+	5.2	1.5	15.4	1.7
5%-	7.2	15.2	3.2	19.7
1%+	1.7	0.2	5.2	0.7
1%-	1.7	4.7	1.0	8.5

Note: In the first two lines we find the percentage of t-values significant at 5% and 1%, respectively. In the last four lines the positive (negative) signs indicate that the we calculate the percentage of positive (negative) t-values that are larger than the one-tail critical value at the given significance level.

working with short series. As an example, we provide the same test for autocorrelation with our data aggregated from four-digit to two-digit sectors. Needless to say, aggregated data is what we usually find in empirical macroeconomic research in most economic journals. The results of such a tests are reported in Table 3.16. They give, as before, the t-values of the AR(1) and AR(2) coefficients of a regression of the residuals of both equations, estimated with individual time series of aggregated SRs and DSRs. The estimates of the parameters are omitted, since we are only interested in showing how such a test would be unable to reject the null of no autocorrelation, when in fact it can be seen by pooling more disaggregated data that some precautions against autocorrelation have to be taken. The approach of pooling disaggregated data is more efficient and gives much more information than the standard work with aggregated variables.

Final Estimated Markups with Sectoral Instruments.

Since there is some indication of an AR(2) in a group of series of residuals in both equations, we re-calculate the standard errors of the estimated coefficients by making their variance-covariance matrix robust to second order autocorrelation as well as heteroskedasticity and cross-correlation between sectors. Point estimates remain the same; only the standard errors change.

Tables 3.17 and 3.18 contain in the first four columns the PCM estimated with our final set of instrumental variables (but with OLS for sectors 21, 27, 28 and 31) and the new robust standard errors. It is apparent that the new standard errors are almost at the same level as the previous ones, and they are even lower than before in some cases. Our estimates of markups are as efficient as with standard errors which are robust only in front of heteroskedasticity.

There are two main features which are worth pointing out in the tables. First, leaving aside sector 31 Leather, which has a significantly negative estimated margin, most other sectors have price-cost margins which are positive and range between 18% and 50% (with a few exceptions: 21 Tobacco, 23 Apparel, 24 Lumber and Wood and 29 Petroleum and Coal in the SR equation). Standard errors are very low, due to the large number of data points used in the estimation. Using the SR equation as a benchmark (for purposes of comparison with other authors), we can observe that on average markups for durables are higher than for non-durables,[10] and that there is a core of industries with high and and relatively similar levels of margins (around 35%). These are still high values, especially if we take into account that we have corrected the measure of labor share, thus eliminating part of the bias produced by the use of establishments instead of firms. Norrbin, when correcting Hall's data for the labor share and materials share, obtains markups of around 1.10, although the data set he uses is more aggregated than the one used here. Our results confirm qualitatively those of Domowitz et al. (1988) even after the adjustment of the labor share.

Second, margins calculated with the SR are close to those obtained with the DSR. This similarity is remarkable, since it is obtained using very different data (quantities on the one hand and prices on the other), and it reinforces the evidence in favor of the existence of high markups. However, the SR equation yields slightly higher margins than the DSR equation in almost all sectors. The systematic difference between both equations can be an indication of any phenomenon that makes the SR more procyclical than the DSR. It seems that effort variations not compensated in a period-by-period basis might be a plausible explanation of such a pattern, although a closer look at this bias will be taken in Chapter 5.

Hall claims in his article that labor hoarding is not an alternative to margins in explaining the failure of the exogeneity of the SR. This is due to the fact that when firms hoard labor, their marginal cost is very low (because firms with excess labor capacity can increase production from a low level at almost no cost), and competition would force them to lower prices, thus increasing the revenue share of labor and eliminating the bias produced by the slow adjustment of labor. But it is possible, as Hall recognizes, that labor hoarding goes together with rigid prices (keeping prices equal to average cost in order to avoid losses). This implies that the margin of price over marginal cost is countercyclical, revealing a non-competitive behavior. It also implies that the labor share remains constant and therefore labor hoarding induces a spurious SR. The fact that shares do not vary much in time gives a hint of this countercyclical behavior of markups. In our framework, the combination of labor hoarding and countercyclical markups may produce a bias in the estimation of μ in the SR equation, since the slow adjustment of labor when output changes is not accomodated by fluctuations in the labor share. We will examine further in Chapter 5 possible the biases induced on the SR and the DSR by labor hoarding.

Given that the difference between both estimates is usually less than 0.1, we try to exploit jointly the information on prices and quantities and estimate a single markup parameter by pooling both equations. For each two-digit industry, we use a different intercept for each four-digit sector *and* each equation, but we restrict the margins parameter to be the same for both equations and all sectors. The results can be found in the last two columns of Tables 3.17 and 3.18. They confirm that durables' margins are larger than non-durables', and that their standard errors are very small. The only exception among durables industries is 24 Lumber and Wood products, which has a price-cost margin indistinguishable from 0 at the 5% significance level.

The evidence for non-durables is mixed. For three industries (26 Paper, 27 Printing and 30 Rubber and Plastic), markups are as high as for durables, and also very efficiently estimated. For three other industries (22 Textile Products, 23 Apparel and 28 Chemicals) there is some evidence of markups, although the SR and the DSR equations give different values, and the pooled estimation is just an average of them. For the remaining three industries the markups estimated are small.

3.5 Aggregate Instruments.

Aggregate instruments for demand have been used extensively in the literature on cyclical movements of productivity.[11] Underlying these studies is the idea that aggregate variables in some way reflect demand shocks, whereas productivity shocks are more likely to be sectoral and possibly extend to other sectors after some lag. Changes in aggregate variables such as the oil price, an index of import prices, Gross National Product (GNP) or defense expenditures should not reflect changes in technology. This assumption has been criticized and it remains the main source of skepticism about the estimation of markups.

On the one hand, it is argued that many growth models rely on aggregate supply shocks as the main source of growth in aggregate production. The idea that changes in GNP reflect technological progress at business cycle frequencies is at the heart of many real business cycle models. In this sense, it can be argued that aggregate GNP is not a valid instrument for demand because it reflects productivity changes. On the other hand, it is more difficult to believe that the other common aggregated instruments (especially oil prices and import prices, much more correlated with sectoral SR's) include a technology component as well.

In this section we apply the overidentification test to some of the most commonly used aggregate instruments of demand: rates of change of oil prices, defence expenditures, an index of import prices and real GNP. We estimate the model with all four instruments (Table 3.19), and test for possible overidentification imposed by each of them (Tables 3.20 and 3.21). The new calculations also serve in assessing the sensitivity of our results to the choice of instruments.

The new results are as follows. For those industries that yielded high margins with the sectoral instruments (25-27, 30, 32-39) we obtain again large values, although here they are slightly smaller than before. For sector 24 Lumber and Wood we find no markups, and the markups for sectors 22 and 23, Textile Mill and Apparel, are larger now. In general we obtain a more homogeneous pattern than we did with sectoral instruments, especially in those sectors for which the model did not seem to work in the previous section, which now give results in line with the other industries. This is the case for sectors 21 Tobacco, 28 Chemicals and 29 Petroleum, although in this latter case standard errors are very large. This suggest that sectoral instrumental variables were not appropriate for these sectors. Finally, the results of sector 31 Leather Products still yield negative and implausible margins.

Looking at the overidentifying restrictions, we see that oil prices fail the test for four industries, while defence expenditures fail for only one, import prices for five and GNP for five. This does not seem to imply a massive rejection of conventional aggregate instruments, especially if we consider that the t-values of the "failing" instruments are not very large. However, for each instrument most sectors' t-values tend to have the same sign, suggesting that overall the aggregate instruments approach is not valid.

3.6 Exogeneity Tests.

The main fact that Hall tried to explain in his 1988 article was the correlation of measured productivity with his instruments of demand. If the SR is a good measure of productivity change, it should not be correlated with variables that are exogenous *a priori*. This exogeneity test failed for most industries with his NIPA data.

In Tables 3.22 and 3.23 we replicate the test for exogeneity of our four-digit productivity measures with respect to two of the main aggregated instruments, oil price changes and the GNP growth rate. We also construct for each sector a series of SRs and DSRs using as weights the revenue shares *corrected* by the markups that we have obtained in our pooling regressions with sectoral instruments. We call them SRc and DSRc. These shares should capture the true elasticities if the markups estimated are correct. Then we look at the correlation of the new productivity measures with the aggregated variables, to check if it has fallen.

The main result that can be observed in the tables is that the correlation of the residuals with GNP growth and oil price changes disappears after we correct them for markups. It is a natural result, since the SRc and DSRc are the residuals of the regression used for their estimation, plus the fixed effect. Our model tries to clean the SR and the DSR of their demand driven component (using sectoral demand instruments), and therefore the corrected residuals are uncorrelated with other demand instruments (in this case aggregate variables). There are a few sectors for which the test of exogeneity of the corrected residuals still fails. But, in general, the new corrected measures of productivity seem to be exogenous to aggregate instruments of demand. In this sense, they appear to be more accurate measures of productivity changes than the uncorrected residuals.

3.7 Conclusion

Markups are one of the central explanations for the procyclicality of observed productivity. We have found high markup values for most US Manufacturing industries. The values obtained, once converted into price-cost margins (the Lerner index) are in many cases above 30%, which far exceeds typical profit rates in American firms. This suggests that increasing returns to scale are probably important (even if our data on capital is not good enough to estimate returns to scale accurately), and that imperfect competition is a key element in explaining procyclical SR. The main alternative explanations of this stylized fact are externalities (which we analyze in the next chapter) and true technological changes over the cycle. We believe that the technology hypothesis is inconsistent with the correlation of the measures of productivity with demand instruments, as Hall has shown in his pioneering article (and we have replicated here with a much richer data set).

We have used information from the SR and the DSR to estimate markups. The markups obtained with each residual are very similar, which makes our estimates more reliable. The margins calculated with the SR are slightly higher than those calculated with the DSR. We have argued that this difference can be explained by labor hoarding. In any case, the magnitude of this effect is not large enough to explain the whole of the markup.

Our investigation with the SR and the DSR provides an explanation as to the sources of fluctuations which differs to the ones provided by Shapiro (1987) and Roeger (1995). In the first of these papers it is argued that the similarity of the SR and the DSR indicates that demand shock and markups cannot explain their behavior at high frequencies. The second paper estimates the level of markups, but still defends the hypothesis that demand has no role in driving the economy. Here we have shown that demand and oil shocks are a more plausible explanation of the productivity puzzle, given the comovement of the SR and the DSR with aggregate instruments of demand. A combination of demand and oil shocks, accommodated by markup pricing, can produce a SR and a DSR positively correlated with each other and with the business cycle even if the rate of technological progress is constant.

These findings are closely related to the result given in Rotemberg and Woodford (1992) that oil prices are correlated with real wages and employment. In their paper they show how markups can account for the observed negative correlation of oil prices and real wages. Standard competitive theories imply that oil shocks do not substantially affect real wages, because these shocks do not shift the labor demand curve. In our study, we have seen that the DSR moves with oil prices under imperfect competition. If we view the DSR as a sort of extended rate of growth of real wages (a real wage corrected by the growth rates of other inputs' prices), our results seem compatible with theirs.

Notes

[1]This section closely follows Shapiro's derivation and notation, although we extend it to allow for markups and returns to scale.

[2]Countercyclical markups have become one of the leading New-keynesian explanations of business cycles, since they give a rationale for the behavior of real wages. See Rotemberg and Woodford (1991) for an overview. A recent calibrated model of business cycles which relies solely on cyclical markups is Basu (1995).

[3]Shapiro uses a value-added production function. The DSR constructed with value added data also shifts when materials prices move and markups exist, because the value-added deflator calculated with revenue shares as weights will move with materials prices when price exceeds marginal cost. This spurious change will come up as a negative DSR when materials prices increase, adding to the effect we describe here.

[4]The assumption of white noise disturbances (SR* and DSR*) is needed for the calculation of the standard errors of the markups. But, strictly speaking, for obtaining consistent estimates of the markups the only requirement is that true technology changes are uncorrelated with the instruments we will use, as Hall (1988) has shown.

[5]As stressed by Morrison (1992).

[6]For instance, papers by Domowitz et al. (1988), Caballero and Lyons (1992), Bartelsman, Caballero and Lyons (1994), Norrbin (1993), Basu and Fernald (1994) and (1995) and Waldmann (1991) use the same set of instruments, in some cases with one lag. GNP growth and import prices are sometimes included as well.

[7]For a more detailed discussion of these instruments, see Hall (1988). Bailey (1990) is a good example of the criticisms of aggregate instruments.

[8]Hall (1990) and Caballero and Lyons (1992) approach the estimation of the degree of returns to scale (internal or external to the firm) in a different way, i.e. using cost shares to construct Solow

residuals instead of revenue shares. In this way they manage to avoid linking γ to the coefficient of capital. The degree of returns to scale is implicitly given in their case by the ratio of the sum of elasticities to the profit rate.

[9]Another possibility is to take the output growth rates of the unrelated sectors, instead of the residuals. However, the results hardly change with these alternative instruments.

[10]Recall that durables correspond to industries 24 Lumber-Wood, 25 Furniture, 32 Stone-Glass, 33 Primary Metals, 34 Fabricated Metals, 35 Machinery, 36 Electric Machinery, 37 Transportation Equipment, 38 Instruments and 39 Miscellaneous.

[11]See note 6 in this chapter.

Appendix 1: Derivation of Equation (3.4): Dual Solow Residual with Predetermined Capital

Here we derive the DSR for a Cobb-Douglas production function when capital is determined one period in advance. We omit time subscripts. The Cobb-Douglas function with returns to scale of degree γ takes the form:

$$Y = A \left[N^{\alpha}\, M^{\beta}\, K^{(1-\alpha-\beta)}\right]^{\gamma}$$

Cost minimization conditions for labour and materials are

$$F_N = \gamma\, \alpha\, \frac{Y}{N} = \frac{W}{MC}$$
$$F_M = \gamma\, \beta\, \frac{Y}{M} = \frac{V}{MC}$$

Capital is fixed. Substituting N and M from these conditions into the production function yields

$$Y = \left[\left(\gamma\alpha\, Y\, \frac{MC}{W}\right)^{\alpha} \left(\gamma\beta\, Y\, \frac{MC}{V}\right)^{\beta} K^{(1-\alpha-\beta)}\right]^{\gamma} A$$

From here we can obtain the productivity index as

$$A = Y^{(1-\gamma\alpha-\gamma\beta)} \left(\frac{\alpha}{W}\right)^{-\gamma\alpha} \left(\frac{\beta}{V}\right)^{-\gamma\beta} (\gamma\, MC)^{-\gamma(\alpha+\beta)}\, K^{-\gamma(1-\alpha-\beta)}$$

We difference the logarithm of A to obtain true productivity change $DSR^{*} \equiv a$. As in the derivation in the text (Section 3.1.2), we assume that markups are constant (such that $p = mc$)

$$\begin{aligned} DSR^{*} &= (1-\gamma\alpha-\gamma\beta)\, y + \gamma\alpha\, w + \gamma\beta\, v - \\ &\quad -\gamma(\alpha+\beta)\, p - \gamma\, (1-\alpha-\beta)\, k \\ &= \gamma\alpha\, (w-p) + \gamma\beta\, (v-p) + \\ &\quad +(1-\gamma\alpha-\gamma\beta)\, (y-k) + (\gamma-1)\, k \end{aligned}$$

We have seen in Section 3.1.1 that the elasticity of the production function with respect to each factor is equal to μ times its revenue share. The elasticities of the Cobb-Douglas production function are

$$\varepsilon_N = \gamma\alpha = \mu\ S_N$$
$$\varepsilon_M = \gamma\beta = \mu\ S_M$$

We can thus rewrite the residual as

$$DSR^* = \mu S_N\ (w-p)+\mu S_M\ (v-p)+(1-\mu S_N-\mu S_M)\ (y-k)+(\gamma-1)\ k$$

Appendix 2: Sectoral Instrumental Variables

The following list of sectors has been taken from Jimeno (1989). It indicates the SIC numbers of those two-digit sectors that are not related to each other through input linkages. His calculations are based on averages over the whole period (1952-1986). It seems reasonable to assume that they do not change for our time period (1958-84).

The instruments used originally were the aggregated (over 4-digit sub-sectors) SRs of each 2-digit sector, for the SR equations, and the correponding DSRs for the DSR equations. As Jimeno points out, sectors 21, 23, 25 and 31 appear repeatedly as suitable instruments, since their production goes mainly to final demand.

- 21 Tobacco: 23 25 31 35 36 37
- 22 Textile: 21 25 31 37
- 23 Apparel: 21 36 37
- 24 Lumber-Wood: 21 23 31
- 25 Furniture: 21 31
- 26 Paper: 21 25 31
- 27 Printing: 21 23 25 31 37
- 28 Chemicals: 21 23 25 31
- 29 Petroleum-Coal: 21 23 25 31 37
- 30 Rubber-Plastic: 21 23 31
- 31 Leather: 21 25 36 37
- 32 Stone-Clay-Glass: 21 23 25 31
- 33 Primary Metals: 21 23 25 31
- 34 Fabricated Metals: 21 23 25 31
- 35 Machinery: 21 23 25 31
- 36 Electric Machinery: 21 23 31
- 37 Transportation Equipment: 21 31
- 38 Instruments: 21 31
- 39 Miscellaneous: 21 31

Appendix 3: Tables of Results

Table 3.3: *Preliminary estimation of margins and returns to scale.*

	SR equation				DSR equation			
	PCM	s.e.	γ	s.e.	PCM	s.e.	γ	s.e.
21	-1.34	1.16	0.03	0.39	-3.21	3.03	-0.10	0.42
22	0.23	0.06	1.05	0.09	0.07	0.07	0.88	0.06
23	0.26	0.07	1.02	0.08	0.24	0.07	1.06	0.05
24	-0.06	0.07	0.74	0.44	-0.21	0.09	0.59	0.44
25	0.32	0.03	1.37	0.82	0.32	0.03	0.76	0.49
26	0.10	0.20	2.39	0.70	0.16	0.18	2.62	0.96
27	0.42	0.04	1.39	0.35	0.31	0.08	0.92	0.65
28	0.56	0.08	4.12	2.61	0.39	0.11	3.81	2.24
29	0.36	0.19	0.14	2.54	0.27	0.28	-1.51	4.86
30	0.36	0.04	1.23	0.46	0.32	0.03	1.08	0.44
31	-1.11	0.63	-0.72	0.70	-1.00	0.52	-0.49	0.63
32	0.36	0.07	-1.54	3.76	0.29	0.03	0.71	0.98
33	0.22	0.08	2.44	1.88	0.13	0.15	3.30	2.98
34	0.32	0.03	1.50	0.54	0.30	0.05	2.01	0.97
35	0.40	0.04	0.87	1.12	0.29	0.05	0.59	0.86
36	0.30	0.04	0.46	0.63	0.28	0.03	0.70	0.37
37	0.21	0.04	0.80	0.40	0.19	0.03	0.83	0.29
38	0.30	0.10	-0.57	1.04	0.19	0.09	-0.45	0.91
39	0.42	0.08	1.79	0.95	0.37	0.09	1.78	0.81

Note: Instrumental variables estimations with sectoral instruments. Fixed effects were used for pooling four-digit SIC sectors within two-digit sectors. The first stage of 2SLS was done also with fixed effects. Heteroskedasticity-consistent standard errors were applied. Markups are transformed into price-cost margins (PCM).

Table 3.4: *Labour, materials and capital: Average growth rate and its standard deviation.*

SIC	Labour	s.e.	Materials	s.e.	Capital	s. e.
21	-0.028	0.080	-0.016	0.093	0.029	0.065
22	-0.001	0.117	0.031	0.161	0.033	0.226
23	0.001	0.113	0.024	0.167	0.030	0.161
24	0.013	0.120	0.032	0.128	0.029	0.049
25	0.023	0.138	0.042	0.182	0.041	0.047
26	0.004	0.079	0.034	0.175	0.032	0.045
27	0.014	0.093	0.033	0.128	0.045	0.064
28	0.008	0.086	0.041	0.108	0.038	0.044
29	0.009	0.111	0.038	0.133	0.050	0.059
30	0.004	0.099	0.031	0.144	0.022	0.040
31	-0.020	0.089	-0.005	0.108	0.005	0.065
32	-0.004	0.094	0.022	0.120	0.018	0.038
33	0.004	0.103	0.036	0.172	0.031	0.057
34	0.018	0.118	0.038	0.174	0.035	0.062
35	0.011	0.097	0.039	0.143	0.040	0.036
36	0.021	0.115	0.056	0.238	0.051	0.086
37	0.019	0.145	0.048	0.210	0.036	0.072
38	0.025	0.101	0.049	0.131	0.055	0.036
39	-0.002	0.100	0.021	0.117	0.042	0.060

Note: The average is unweighted and it is over four-digit sectors and time. The standard deviations are the square root of average variances over four-digit sectors.

Table 3.5: *Estimation of markups with the original instruments.*

	SR equation		DSR equation	
	PCM	s.e.	PCM	s.e.
21 Tobacco	-2.39	2.26	-1.17	1.14
22 Textile Mill	0.21	0.06	0.10	0.07
23 Apparel	0.14	0.09	0.20	0.07
24 Lumber-Wood	0.01	0.06	-0.12	0.08
25 Furniture	0.36	0.02	0.32	0.02
26 Paper	0.36	0.05	0.29	0.03
27 Printing	0.36	0.05	0.26	0.10
28 Chemicals	0.48	0.07	0.31	0.08
29 Petroleum-Coal	0.12	0.13	-0.23	0.45
30 Rubber-Plastic	0.37	0.04	0.31	0.03
31 Leather	-1.16	0.79	-0.31	0.33
32 Stone-Glass	0.37	0.02	0.31	0.03
33 Primary Metals	0.26	0.03	0.10	0.05
34 Fabr. Metals	0.35	0.03	0.28	0.02
35 Machinery	0.45	0.03	0.32	0.03
36 Electric Machinery	0.33	0.03	0.29	0.02
37 Transportation Equipment	0.29	0.03	0.24	0.03
38 Instruments	0.49	0.07	0.35	0.04
39 Miscellaneous	0.47	0.07	0.37	0.05

Note: Instrumental variables estimations with sectoral instruments. Fixed effects were used for pooling four-digit SIC sectors within two-digit sectors. The first stage of 2SLS was done also with fixed effects. Heteroskedasticity-consistent standard errors were applied. Markups are transformed into price-cost margins (PCM).

Table 3.6: *Overidentification test for original instruments in the SR equation: t-values (main row) and sectors used as instruments (row below).*

21	-0.228	1.255	0.527	1.987	-0.211	0.266
	23	25	31	35	36	37
22	1.756	-0.785	0.184	-0.027		
	21	25	31	37		
23	-0.040	2.344	0.725			
	21	36	37			
24	-0.373	3.389	-0.653			
	21	23	31			
25	-0.720	1.077				
	21	31				
26	1.966	4.252	3.491			
	21	25	31			
27	-0.123	1.692	2.467	2.676	1.166	
	21	23	25	31	37	
28	6.087	1.732	3.914	4.618		
	21	23	25	31		
29	1.541	0.728	0.319	1.497	1.715	
	21	23	25	31	37	
30	0.427	0.712	1.015			
	21	23	31			
31	-2.610	0.508	0.616	-2.802		
	21	25	36	37		
32	3.033	3.699	1.014	4.011		
	21	23	25	31		
33	0.908	2.170	1.475	4.149		
	21	23	25	31		
34	1.724	1.958	2.478	2.873		
	21	23	25	31		
35	1.149	2.416	1.486	1.112		
	21	23	25	31		
36	1.058	-0.200	0.254			
	21	23	31			
37	-1.846	1.048				
	21	31				
38	1.695	2.149				
	21	31				
39	0.121	2.659				
	21	31				

Table 3.7: *Overidentification test for original instruments in the DSR equation: t-values (main row) and sectors used as instruments (row below).*

21	-1.116	1.764	0.728	1.608	0.468	0.175
	23	25	31	35	36	37
22	3.128	-1.117	-1.889	-1.908		
	21	25	31	37		
23	0.548	2.185	-0.442			
	21	36	37			
24	1.219	8.412	-1.078			
	21	23	31			
25	-0.305	0.202				
	21	31				
26	8.133	4.977	1.909			
	21	25	31			
27	0.935	0.661	3.512	2.016	0.684	
	21	23	25	31	37	
28	5.429	-2.574	4.290	3.622		
	21	23	25	31		
29	1.354	0.376	1.259	1.751	1.296	
	21	23	25	31	37	
30	0.388	0.225	-0.266			
	21	23	31			
31	-1.394	0.205	1.093	-2.023		
	21	25	36	37		
32	-1.719	2.658	1.733	5.578		
	21	23	25	31		
33	1.517	1.035	3.328	2.648		
	21	23	25	31		
34	1.863	0.823	2.783	3.559		
	21	23	25	31		
35	1.916	0.263	3.137	2.679		
	21	23	25	31		
36	-0.993	-0.103	0.652			
	21	23	31			
37	-2.756	0.729				
	21	31				
38	0.466	0.559				
	21	31				
39	-0.310	1.983				
	21	31				

Table 3.8: *Re-estimation of markups with instruments that pass the overidentification test in both equations at the same time.*

	SR equation		DSR equation	
	PCM	s.e.	PCM	s.e.
21 Tobacco	6.21	6.84	-1.25	1.20
22 Textile Mill	0.18	0.05	0.03	0.09
23 Apparel	0.08	0.11	0.17	0.08
24 Lumber-Wood	0.02	0.06	-0.09	0.07
25 Furniture	0.36	0.02	0.32	0.02
26 Paper	0.44	0.09	0.25	0.04
27 Printing	0.29	0.06	0.26	0.10
28 Chemicals	-0.49	0.83	0.42	0.08
29 Petroleum-Coal	0.12	0.13	-0.23	0.45
30 Rubber-Plastic	0.37	0.04	0.31	0.03
31 Leather	-0.63	0.50	-0.21	0.35
32 Stone-Glass	0.36	0.02	0.31	0.03
33 Primary Metals	0.36	0.17	191.27	190.92
34 Fabr. Metals	0.32	0.08	0.26	0.03
35 Machinery	0.77	0.18	0.13	0.19
36 Electric Machinery	0.33	0.03	0.29	0.02
37 Transportation Equipment	0.29	0.03	0.25	0.03
38 Instruments	0.49	0.07	0.35	0.04
39 Miscellaneous	0.38	0.09	0.26	0.11

Note: Instrumental variables estimations with sectoral instruments. Fixed effects were used for pooling four-digit SIC sectors within two-digit sectors. The first stage of 2SLS was done also with fixed effects. Heteroskedasticity-consistent standard errors were applied. Markups are transformed into price-cost margins (PCM).

Table 3.9: R^2 *of 1st stage and* χ^2 *test for the significance of the instruments in the 1st stage. New common instruments.*

	SR equation			DSR equation		
SIC	R^2	χ^2 test	dg fr	R^2	χ^2 test	dg fr
21	0.04	2.27	5	0.07	3.94	5
22	0.08	18.34	3	0.09	29.28	3
23	0.06	6.46	2	0.06	9.52	2
24	0.30	166.35	2	0.30	168.42	2
25	0.16	55.13	2	0.18	64.98	2
26	0.06	11.82	2	0.10	28.26	2
27	0.07	21.96	3	0.10	30.76	3
28	0.04	5.65	1	0.05	22.65	1
29	0.12	8.52	5	0.14	10.71	5
30	0.19	28.53	3	0.23	40.47	3
31	0.05	9.44	2	0.04	6.39	2
32	0.22	167.30	1	0.20	139.33	1
33	0.09	7.28	1	0.07	3.06	1
34	0.04	14.31	2	0.07	48.18	2
35	0.02	0.49	1	0.03	15.91	1
36	0.12	118.67	3	0.18	187.20	3
37	0.09	33.26	1	0.07	28.07	1
38	0.05	11.55	2	0.09	27.65	2
39	0.09	15.26	1	0.08	9.64	1

Note: The χ^2 is a test for the joint significance of the slopes in the first stage of 2SLS estimation. The expression 'dg fr' refers to the degrees of freedom.

Table 3.10: *Re-estimation of markups with new instruments, different for each equation.*

	SR equation		DSR equation	
	PCM	s.e.	PCM	s.e.
21 Tobacco	6.21	6.84	-1.17	1.14
22 Textile Mill	0.21	0.06	0.03	0.09
23 Apparel	0.08	0.11	0.17	0.08
24 Lumber-Wood	0.02	0.06	-0.09	0.07
25 Furniture	0.36	0.02	0.32	0.02
26 Paper	0.49	0.19	0.34	0.06
27 Printing	0.29	0.06	0.26	0.10
28 Chemicals	-0.49	0.83	0.42	0.08
29 Petroleum-Coal	0.12	0.13	-0.23	0.45
30 Rubber-Plastic	0.37	0.04	0.31	0.03
31 Leather	-0.63	0.50	-0.08	0.29
32 Stone-Glass	0.36	0.02	0.32	0.03
33 Primary Metals	0.25	0.03	0.02	0.09
34 Fabricated Metals	0.32	0.08	0.26	0.03
35 Machinery	0.47	0.03	0.30	0.05
36 Electric Machinery	0.33	0.03	0.29	0.02
37 Transportation Equipment	0.29	0.03	0.25	0.03
38 Instruments	0.49	0.07	0.35	0.04
39 Miscellaneous	0.38	0.09	0.26	0.11

Note: Instrumental variables estimations with sectoral instruments. Fixed effects were used for pooling four-digit SIC sectors within two-digit sectors. The first stage of 2SLS was done also with fixed effects. Heteroskedasticity-consistent standard errors were applied. Markups are transformed into price-cost margins (PCM).

Table 3.11: *Overidentification test for the new independent instruments. SR equation: t-values (main row) and sectors used as instruments (row below).*

21	-0.130	0.638	0.282	-0.443	0.014
	23	25	31	36	37
22	1.756	-0.785	0.184	-0.027	
	21	25	31	37	
23	0.011	0.738			
	21	37			
24	-0.387	-0.704			
	21	31			
25	-0.720	1.077			
	21	31			
26	3.148				
	21				
27	0.429	1.117	1.417		
	21	23	37		
28	0.949				
	23				
29	1.541	0.728	0.319	1.497	1.715
	21	23	25	31	37
30	0.427	0.712	1.015		
	21	23	31		
31	-0.296	0.207			
	25	36			
32	2.680				
	25				
33	0.861	2.411			
	21	25			
34	2.131	0.593			
	21	23			
35	1.090	0.589	0.505		
	21	25	31		
36	1.058	-0.200	0.254		
	21	23	31		
37	-1.846	1.048			
	21	31			
38	1.695	2.149			
	21	31			
39	1.086				
	21				

Table 3.12: *Overidentification test for the new instruments. DSR equation: t-values (main row) and sectors used as instruments (row below).*

21	-1.116	1.764	0.728	1.608	0.468	0.175
	23	25	31	35	36	37
22	-0.790	-1.571	-1.621			
	25	31	37			
23	0.613	-0.417				
	21	37				
24	1.067	-2.026				
	21	31				
25	-0.305	0.202				
	21	31				
26	2.361					
	31					
27	0.931	0.649	0.682			
	21	23	37			
28	-1.693					
	23					
29	1.354	0.376	1.259	1.751	1.296	
	21	23	25	31	37	
30	0.388	0.225	-0.266			
	21	23	31			
31	-1.360	-0.220	0.847			
	21	25	36			
32	-1.712	1.625				
	21	25				
33	1.344	0.026				
	21	23				
34	1.236	-0.337				
	21	23				
35	1.397	0.335				
	21	23				
36	-0.993	-0.103	0.652			
	21	23	31			
37	0.173					
	31					
38	0.466	0.559				
	21	31				
39	0.566					
	21					

Table 3.13: R^2 *of 1st stage and* χ^2 *test for the significance of the instruments in the 1st stage. New independent instruments.*

	SR equation			DSR equation		
SIC	R^2	χ^2 test	dg fr	R^2	χ^2 test	dg fr
21	0.04	2.27	5	0.07	3.94	6
22	0.08	19.34	4	0.09	29.28	3
23	0.06	6.46	2	0.06	9.52	2
24	0.30	166.35	2	0.30	168.42	2
25	0.16	55.13	2	0.18	64.98	2
26	0.04	1.96	1	0.09	24.44	1
27	0.07	21.96	3	0.10	30.76	3
28	0.04	5.65	1	0.05	22.65	1
29	0.12	8.52	5	0.14	10.71	5
30	0.19	28.53	3	0.23	40.47	3
31	0.05	9.44	2	0.04	7.66	3
32	0.22	167.30	1	0.20	142.51	2
33	0.23	132.55	2	0.16	69.64	2
34	0.04	14.31	2	0.07	48.18	2
35	0.13	131.31	3	0.09	88.28	2
36	0.12	118.67	3	0.18	187.20	3
37	0.09	33.29	2	0.07	28.07	1
38	0.05	11.55	2	0.09	27.65	2
39	0.09	15.26	1	0.08	9.64	1

Note: The χ^2 is a test for the joint significance of the slopes in the first stage of 2SLS estimation. The expression 'dg fr' refers to the degrees of freedom.

Table 3.14: *Estimation of markups with OLS.*

	SR equation		DSR equation	
	PCM	s.e.	PCM	s.e.
21 Tobacco	0.06	0.09	0.06	0.09
22 Textile Mill	0.14	0.02	0.16	0.01
23 Apparel	0.15	0.03	0.17	0.01
24 Lumber-Wood	0.05	0.04	0.00	0.04
25 Furniture	0.28	0.02	0.24	0.01
26 Paper	0.02	0.07	0.13	0.03
27 Printing	0.25	0.02	0.10	0.12
28 Chemicals	0.22	0.04	0.16	0.03
29 Petroleum-Coal	-0.01	0.06	-0.04	0.06
30 Rubber-Plastic	0.19	0.04	0.22	0.02
31 Leather	0.04	0.04	0.03	0.04
32 Stone-Glass	0.24	0.02	0.20	0.02
33 Primary Metals	0.09	0.03	0.03	0.04
34 Fabr. Metals	0.17	0.02	0.18	0.01
35 Machinery	0.26	0.02	0.22	0.01
36 Electric Mach.	0.12	0.05	0.18	0.02
37 Transp. Equip.	0.17	0.03	0.14	0.01
38 Instruments	0.22	0.02	0.21	0.02
39 Miscellaneous	0.21	0.03	0.18	0.04

Note: Fixed effects and heteroskedasticity-consistent standard errors were applied.

Table 3.15: *Test for AR(2) of the residuals pooling the data with fixed effects.*

	SR equation				DSR equation			
	AR1	t	AR2	t	AR1	t	AR2	t
21	0.04	0.37	-0.01	-0.11	0.09	0.93	-0.03	-0.26
22	-0.06	-1.73	-0.12	-3.22	0.06	1.76	-0.15	-4.50
23	-0.06	-1.77	-0.21	-5.61	0.00	0.05	-0.15	-3.95
24	-0.11	-2.29	-0.17	-3.33	-0.08	-1.73	-0.20	-4.15
25	-0.08	-1.51	-0.16	-2.81	-0.01	-0.20	-0.22	-4.04
26	-0.08	-1.71	-0.14	-4.34	0.11	2.30	-0.27	-5.94
27	0.01	0.20	-0.16	-3.24	-0.23	-4.50	-0.14	-2.86
28	0.00	0.18	-0.14	-3.57	0.14	3.67	-0.13	-3.21
29	0.16	1.73	-0.18	-1.93	0.09	1.06	-0.21	-2.37
30	0.14	1.64	-0.08	-0.97	0.29	3.46	-0.12	-1.45
31	-0.01	-0.29	-0.03	-0.64	-0.03	-0.52	-0.13	-2.23
32	-0.11	-2.79	-0.16	-3.92	0.17	4.39	-0.21	-5.10
33	-0.15	-3.76	-0.09	-2.36	-0.05	-1.26	-0.12	-3.13
34	0.02	0.60	-0.05	-1.80	0.12	3.69	-0.15	-4.41
35	0.05	1.62	-0.00	-0.01	0.18	5.89	-0.01	-0.47
36	-0.05	-1.79	-0.06	-2.42	0.11	3.62	-0.02	-0.94
37	-0.04	-0.82	-0.16	-3.18	0.15	3.03	-0.15	-3.09
38	0.05	0.99	-0.04	-0.81	0.04	0.67	-0.07	-1.25
39	-0.17	-3.64	-0.15	-3.23	-0.08	-1.73	-0.17	-3.50

Note: Slope coefficients and t-values of the regression of the residuals of the final estimation (those of Table 3.10 with the exception of sectors 21, 28, 29 and 31, for which we use the OLS residuals, in Table 3.14) on their past values. 'AR1' and 'AR2' indicate, respectively, the first and second order autocorrelation coefficients.

Table 3.16: *AR(2) test of the residuals with aggregated data: t-values.*

	SR equation		DSR equation	
	t AR1	t AR2	t AR1	t AR2
21 Tobacco	2.760	-0.675	2.715	-0.667
22 Textile Mill	-1.324	0.273	-0.563	-0.001
23 Apparel	1.602	-0.072	1.393	-0.132
24 Lumber-Wood	0.594	-1.060	0.541	-1.118
25 Furniture	-0.564	0.885	-0.862	0.975
26 Paper	1.150	-1.482	-0.011	-0.889
27 Printing	0.623	-2.002	0.367	-1.169
28 Chemicals	0.428	-0.427	0.623	-0.522
29 Petroleum-Coal	0.984	-0.002	0.638	0.046
30 Rubber-Plastic	0.764	0.623	0.767	0.655
31 Leather	-0.555	-1.344	-0.561	-1.345
32 Stone-Glass	2.199	-1.285	2.170	-0.618
33 Primary Metals	-0.200	-0.728	-0.052	-0.250
34 Fabr. Metals	-0.249	-0.571	0.251	-0.261
35 Machinery	2.967	1.799	1.960	2.161
36 Electric Mach.	1.836	-2.079	0.114	-1.839
37 Transp. Equipment	1.611	-0.564	1.374	-0.226
38 Instruments	0.472	-1.517	0.008	-1.118
39 Miscellaneous	-0.579	-2.284	-0.562	-2.288

Note: Slope coefficients and t-values of the regression on past values of the residuals of the estimation of markups with data aggregated at two-digit level. 'AR1' refers to the first autocorrelation coefficient and 'AR2' to the second.

Table 3.17: *Final estimation of markups. Standard errors robust to heteroskedasticity and AR(2). Sectors estimated with 2SLS.*

	SR eqn		DSR eqn		Pooled eqn	
	PCM	s.e.	PCM	s.e.	PCM	s.e.
22 Textile Mill	0.21	0.03	0.03	0.04	0.13	0.00
23 Apparel	0.08	0.11	0.17	0.10	0.12	0.11
24 Lumber-Wood	0.02	0.04	-0.09	0.02	-0.04	0.02
25 Furniture	0.36	0.02	0.32	0.01	0.35	0.02
26 Paper	0.49	0.20	0.34	0.05	0.66	0.20
27 Printing	0.29	0.06	0.26	0.12	0.24	0.10
30 Rubber-Plastic	0.37	0.05	0.31	0.02	0.34	0.04
32 Stone-Glass	0.36	0.01	0.32	0.03	0.34	0.02
33 Primary Metals	0.25	0.02	0.02	0.06	0.20	0.01
34 Fabr. Metals	0.32	0.09	0.26	0.04	0.32	0.09
35 Machinery	0.47	0.02	0.30	0.04	0.43	0.01
36 Electric Mach.	0.33	0.04	0.29	0.02	0.31	0.03
37 Transp. Equip.	0.29	0.03	0.25	0.01	0.26	0.00
38 Instruments	0.49	0.05	0.35	0.02	0.41	0.03
39 Miscellaneous	0.38	0.04	0.26	0.10	0.33	0.06

Note: Fixed effects were used for pooling four-digit SIC sectors within two-digit sectors. Heteroskedasticity and AR(2)-consistent standard errors were applied. Markups are transformed into price-cost margins (PCM).

Table 3.18: *Final estimation of markups. Standard errors robust to heteroskedasticity and AR(2). Sectors estimated with OLS.*

	SR eqn		DSR eqn		Pooled eqn	
	PCM	s.e.	PCM	s.e.	PCM	s.e.
21. Tobacco	0.06	0.08	0.06	0.10	0.06	0.09
28. Chemicals	0.22	0.03	0.16	0.04	0.19	0.03
29. Petrol-Coal	-0.01	0.05	-0.04	0.08	-0.03	0.06
31. Leather	-0.63	0.03	0.03	0.03	0.03	0.31

Note: Fixed effects were used for pooling four-digit SIC sectors within two-digit sectors. Heteroskedasticity and AR(2)-consistent standard errors were applied. Markups are transformed into price-cost margins (PCM).

Table 3.19: *Estimation of markups with aggregate instruments.*

	SR eqn		DSR eqn	
	PCM	s.e.	PCM	s.e.
21 Tobacco	0.28	0.16	0.35	0.15
22 Textile Mill	0.22	0.05	0.10	0.06
23 Apparel	0.25	0.07	0.23	0.07
24 Lumber and Wood	-0.04	0.06	-0.18	0.07
25 Furniture	0.32	0.03	0.32	0.02
26 Paper	0.16	0.08	0.21	0.04
27 Printing	0.41	0.04	0.31	0.06
28 Chemicals	0.49	0.04	0.31	0.05
29 Petroleum and Coal	0.36	0.18	0.24	0.25
30 Rubber and Plastic	0.36	0.05	0.32	0.04
31 Leather	-0.44	0.34	-0.40	0.27
32 Stone and Glass	0.34	0.02	0.28	0.03
33 Primary Metals	0.20	0.03	0.08	0.06
34 Fabricated Metals	0.31	0.02	0.28	0.03
35 Machinery	0.40	0.02	0.31	0.03
36 Electric Machinery	0.31	0.04	0.28	0.02
37 Transportation Equipment	0.21	0.03	0.20	0.02
38 Instruments	0.38	0.05	0.28	0.04
39 Miscellaneous	0.44	0.07	0.39	0.07

Note: Instrumental variables estimations with sectoral instruments. Fixed effects were used for pooling four-digit SIC sectors within two-digit sectors. The first stage of 2SLS was done also with fixed effects. t-values correspond to the null hypothesis of $\mu = 1$. Heteroskedasticity-consistent standard errors were applied. Markups are transformed into PCM.

Table 3.20: *Overidentification test for aggregate instruments in the SR equation: t-values.*

	Instruments			
	Oil p	Defence	Imp p	GNP
21 Tobacco	-0.24	-1.09	-1.18	1.74
22 Textile Mill	-0.95	1.63	-1.88	0.07
23 Apparel	1.26	-0.38	-1.00	2.13
24 Lumber and Wood	-1.38	0.67	0.52	-1.40
25 Furniture	0.86	-0.79	0.57	0.14
26 Paper	-5.15	0.07	-0.42	3.99
27 Printing	-0.94	0.35	-1.28	0.94
28 Chemicals	-5.25	0.65	-3.31	4.68
29 Petroleum and Coal	-0.76	0.65	0.08	-0.55
30 Rubber and Plastic	0.73	-1.29	-1.04	-0.07
31 Leather	1.57	1.35	5.38	0.22
32 Stone and Glass	-2.84	1.15	-1.28	1.42
33 Primary Metals	-2.15	1.94	-1.12	2.87
34 Fabricated Metals	-1.82	-0.44	1.25	2.01
35 Machinery	-1.80	0.32	-2.93	1.44
36 Electric Machinery	-1.16	-1.12	2.85	2.29
37 Transportation Eqm.	-0.45	-1.16	-1.09	1.16
38 Instruments	-1.08	-2.20	-6.21	1.49
39 Miscellaneous	-0.85	-0.91	-1.29	0.94

Note: The t-value corresponds to the null hypothesis of insignificance of each instrument when added as a regressor in the second stage of the 2SLS estimation.

Table 3.21: *Overidentification test for aggregate instruments in the DSR equation: t-values.*

	Instruments			
	Oil p	Def	Imp p	GNP
21 Tobacco	-0.08	-1.67	-0.33	1.86
22 Textile Mill	-0.59	1.64	0.94	-2.84
23 Apparel	0.39	-1.27	-0.48	1.60
24 Lumber and Wood	-1.56	1.13	0.10	-1.59
25 Furniture	0.28	-0.90	-0.20	-0.18
26 Paper	-4.92	0.40	-1.69	2.63
27 Printing	0.13	-0.25	-0.58	0.08
28 Chemicals	-6.32	0.67	-2.26	4.19
29 Petroleum and Coal	-0.75	1.42	-0.44	0.94
30 Rubber and Plastic	1.39	-0.91	-0.55	-0.24
31 Leather	0.59	0.85	4.41	0.48
32 Stone and Glass	-0.32	0.73	-0.79	0.41
33 Primary Metals	-1.85	1.43	-0.97	2.23
34 Fabricated Metals	-3.68	-0.22	-0.09	3.35
35 Machinery	-2.33	0.22	-0.40	1.87
36 Electric Machinery	-0.53	-1.81	2.30	0.46
37 Transportation Eqm.	-0.67	-1.89	-4.18	2.07
38 Instruments	0.49	-2.03	-0.64	-0.47
39 Miscellaneous	-1.26	-0.38	-0.58	1.06

Note: The t-value corresponds to the null hypothesis of insignificance of each instrument when added as a regressor in the second stage of the 2SLS estimation.

Table 3.22: *Correlations of the SR and the corrected SR (SRc) with aggregate instruments.*

	Correlation with GNP				Correlation with oil price			
	SR	t	SRc	t	SR	t	SRc	t
21	0.42	1.46	0.31	0.58	0.02	0.61	0.09	1.06
22	0.34	2.32	0.02	0.17	-0.05	-1.65	-0.02	-1.03
23	0.33	3.27	0.27	2.68	-0.01	-0.44	0.00	-0.07
24	-0.15	-1.08	-0.18	-1.32	-0.02	-1.07	-0.02	-0.91
25	0.87	4.13	-0.14	-0.93	-0.07	-1.99	0.04	2.86
26	0.51	2.44	-0.39	-1.22	-0.08	-5.02	-0.09	-2.34
27	0.51	3.33	0.23	2.19	-0.03	-1.60	-0.02	-1.32
28	1.10	4.98	1.34	4.75	-0.08	-2.56	-0.07	-1.58
29	0.41	1.43	0.29	0.98	-0.09	-1.33	-0.07	-0.92
30	0.81	3.70	-0.03	-0.15	-0.03	-0.62	0.02	0.99
31	-0.28	-1.53	0.11	0.50	0.04	1.33	0.04	1.28
32	0.87	7.15	0.00	-0.03	-0.08	-3.63	-0.04	-1.61
33	0.81	5.34	-0.07	-0.36	-0.08	-2.49	-0.06	-1.53
34	0.89	6.68	0.01	0.09	-0.07	-3.13	-0.02	-1.55
35	1.21	6.04	-0.25	-1.51	-0.04	-1.15	-0.04	-1.59
36	1.06	5.66	-0.05	-0.36	-0.08	-2.87	-0.02	-0.83
37	0.54	5.29	-0.22	-1.92	-0.05	-2.32	0.01	0.58
38	0.70	4.22	-0.19	-0.85	-0.01	-0.45	-0.03	-0.75
39	0.78	3.62	0.19	0.75	-0.09	-1.62	-0.05	-0.76

Note: SRc were corrected with markups estimated with aggregate instruments. Fixed effects were used for pooling four-digit SIC sectors within two-digit sectors. t-values correspond to the null hypothesis of no correlation between the residuals and aggregate variables. They are calculated with heteroskedasticity-consistent standard errors.

Table 3.23: *Correlations of the DSR and the corrected DSR (DSRc) with aggregate instruments.*

	Correlation with gnp				Correlation with oil p			
	DSR	t	DSRc	t	DSR	t	DSRc	t
21	0.42	1.48	0.37	0.99	0.03	0.92	0.06	1.13
22	0.04	0.27	-0.01	-0.05	-0.03	-1.01	-0.02	-0.91
23	0.28	2.24	0.15	1.24	-0.02	-0.84	0.00	-0.10
24	-0.42	-3.00	-0.24	-1.67	0.01	0.36	-0.01	-0.67
25	0.85	4.89	-0.01	-0.13	-0.08	-2.67	0.01	0.62
26	0.53	3.10	0.07	0.26	-0.09	-4.30	-0.10	-2.44
27	0.38	2.03	0.09	0.53	-0.01	-0.28	0.00	0.03
28	0.81	3.70	0.05	0.17	-0.09	-3.77	-0.11	-2.11
29	0.41	1.05	0.57	1.56	-0.08	-0.74	-0.10	-1.20
30	0.70	3.65	0.02	0.11	-0.02	-0.61	0.03	0.72
31	-0.20	-1.33	-0.14	-0.91	0.00	0.14	0.01	0.26
32	0.69	4.92	-0.10	-0.80	-0.05	-2.29	0.00	0.08
33	0.49	1.70	0.43	1.44	-0.10	-1.93	-0.10	-1.86
34	0.83	6.03	0.17	1.39	-0.08	-3.79	-0.05	-2.46
35	0.97	5.15	0.16	1.08	-0.04	-1.65	-0.05	-3.02
36	0.93	6.41	-0.03	-0.28	-0.06	-2.58	-0.01	-0.43
37	0.51	5.78	-0.12	-1.38	-0.04	-2.64	0.00	0.07
38	0.43	2.92	-0.21	-2.14	0.01	0.46	0.01	0.84
39	0.71	2.98	0.34	1.40	-0.09	-1.86	-0.07	-1.32

Note: DSRc were corrected with markups estimated with aggregate instruments. Fixed effects were used for pooling four-digit SIC sectors within two-digit sectors. t-values correspond to the null hypothesis of no correlation between the residuals and aggregate variables. They are calculated with heteroskedasticity-consistent standard errors.

4

Externalities and the Business Cycle: a VAR Model

4.1 Introduction

In demand-driven macro models, the role of productive externalities has become an important issue, with several implications for the development of economic theory, in both fields of business cycle analysis and growth theory. There are several channels through which economic fluctuations can affect productivity of individual firms. In the Diamond (1982) model, higher levels of aggregate activity result in higher probabilities of matching between compatible agents. This is the leading model of so-called "thick-market" externalities. Temporary demand increases can also induce a permanent reorganization and rationalization of production processes. Learning and knowledge spillovers are another example of how aggregate demand can affect productivity at industry or firm level.

The relevance of productive externalities has also been highlighted by some recent developments in growth theory, based on endogenous technology. In a path-breaking paper, Stadler (1990) has shown how temporary changes in aggregate demand can induce a permanent change in productivity and output levels.[1]

As noted in the first chapter, the empirical investigation of external effects is due to Caballero and Lyons (1990 and 1992), who propose them as another source of procyclical productivity, together with effort variations. Their results for US manufacturing have been challenged by Basu and Fernald (1995) and Marchetti (1994), on the grounds of model misspecifications and data shortcomings; however, Bartelsman, Caballero and Lyons (1994) have provided new evidence on externalities with a highly disaggregated dataset.

In this chapter, we use our data panel to investigate the effects of economic fluctuations on productivity. We use a dynamic model, and analyze over time the response of sectoral productivity to an innovation in aggregate output.

In practice, the analysis of the effect of business cycles on productivity is significantly complicated by measurement errors which typically affect data of labor input. If labor effort varies over the cycle –as Fay and Medoff (1985) and Shea (1992) show– productivity measures can be highly biased and misleading (see for example Abbott et al., 1989, and Gordon, 1990). Positive effort variations result in measured productivity increases, which appear together with true external effects, if any. This is the problem of labor hoarding/effort variations, which we will treat in this chapter and examine more in depth in Chapter 5.

The existing literature has dealt with the problem in two ways: (i) by including proxies for effort among the regressors (see Caballero and Lyons, 1992 and Bartelsman, Caballero and Lyons, 1994), or (ii) by using effort-adjusted measures of productivity growth (see Galí and Hammour, 1993, and Saint-Paul, 1993).[2]

As an alternative to trying to measure effort, we follow Sbordone's (1997) dynamic approach to identify labor hoarding effects separately from productive externalities, while using standard, unadjusted Solow residuals. The method is the following. Within a vector autoregressive model, we simulate an innovation in aggregate activity, which turns out to be highly persistent. We investigate over time the induced change in sectoral productivity induced by that innovation. As time passes, effort variation effects will die out, whereas "true" trading and technological externalities will not vanish. The detection of a persistent positive effect on the productivity level in the long run, therefore, is interpreted as evidence of external effects. This explanation is, like in any structural VAR model, a tag for what it is only temporary and permanent effects of one variable on the other, after the identification assumption is imposed. The degree of confidence on this assumption and on the model that underlies the VAR structure is therefore crucial for accepting that interpretation.

Our findings also help to clarify a closely related issue. Some recent theoretical papers have emphasized the positive effects that recessions may have on productivity, through a number of channels. Caballero and Hammour (1994) have used a model of creative destruction to show that recessions have "cleansing" effects on outdated techniques and products. Hall (1991) has emphasized the role of "organizational" capital, whose accumulation would increase during slumps. These and other studies (see also Bean, 1990, and Aghion and Saint-Paul, 1991) rely on intertemporal substitution of productivity-improving activities along the cycle. Recently, two empirical studies –by Galí and Hammour (1993) and Saint-Paul (1993)– have provided evidence supporting such theories. According to their results, any positive effects of expansions on productivity are more than offset by negative ones, and economic expansions have a negative net effect on productivity in the long run. Our results are quite different. We find that the long-run effect of booms on sectoral productivity is positive in manufacturing as a whole and in most two-digit manufacturing industries (although very close to zero in the remaining industries). In Section 4.3 we suggest a possible explanation for the difference between our results and those cited.

Finally, we perform a number of robustness tests. In particular, we repeat our estimations for each industry at two-digit SIC level, testing the significance of the long-run response of productivity growth to aggregate shocks using the sequential Bonferroni approach. An extension of our base model shows that our results cannot be simply attributed to oil price shocks. We also test if our results are sensitive to the level of aggregation or other features of the data used. Corroborative evidence is found using Jorgenson et al.'s (1987) quality-unadjusted two-digit data.

4.2 A VAR Model of Business Cycles and Productivity

In this section we introduce our basic framework, which follows Sbordone (1997). In order to analyze the dynamic effect of aggregate fluctuations on productivity, we use a vector autoregressive approach.

We characterize the joint dynamics of our main variables –the rate of growth of aggregate economic activity, ΔY, and sectoral productivity, Δs_i– as a stationary two-variable vector autoregressive process of order one. Our measures of the variables are the rate of growth of aggregate manufacturing output, and the sectoral (four-digit level) gross output SR.

More formally, let X(t) be the vector $(\Delta Y, \Delta s_i)$', and u(t) a two-dimensional white noise process. We assume that X(t) follows a stationary stochastic process, with the canonical moving average representation

$$\begin{aligned} X(t) &= \Phi(0)u(t) + \Phi(1)u(t-1) + \Phi(2)u(t-2) + ... \\ &= \sum_{i=0}^{\infty} \Phi(i)u(t-i) \end{aligned}$$

where Var(u)=Ω and $\Phi(0) = I$.[3]

Such a process can also be expressed in terms of orthogonal or fundamental residuals. Let e(t) be the vector $(e_a, e_s)'$, where e_a and e_s are innovations in, respectively, aggregate output and sectoral productivity, and are independent of each other. Then X(t) can be expressed as

$$\begin{aligned} X(t) &= \Theta(0)e(t) + \Theta(1)e(t-1) + \Theta(2)e(t-2) + ... \\ &= \sum_{i=0}^{\infty} \Theta(i)e(t-i) \end{aligned}$$

with Var(e)=I, and where $\Theta(i)$=$\Phi(i)P$, for i=0,1,2...; $e(t) = P^{-1}u(t)$, and the matrix P has to satisfy Ω=PP'.[4]

Since we are interested in the impulse responses of the system (particularly in the response of productivity to innovations in aggregate activity), the identification of such disturbances is a crucial issue. We achieve identification by imposing a Wold-causal chain on ΔY and Δs_i, through a lower Cholesky decomposition of the residual covariance matrix Ω. That is, we assume that the growth of aggregate output may affect contemporaneously sectoral productivity growth, but not vice-versa. This seems a plausible assumption, given the limited size of each sector (either four-digit or two-digit level, depending on the data) vis-à-vis the whole manufacturing sector.

We estimate the model by pooling the 402 four-digit industries in several ways (see next section). In each case, the omission of individual industry effects would result in biased and inconsistent within-group estimates of the parameters. To deal with this problem there are at least two alternative estimating procedures available. If the number of observations is large enough, one can treat individual effects as constants to be estimated, and use the familiar dummy variables least squares estimator, or within-estimator (see for example Hsiao, 1986). The other procedure –which is necessary when the number of observations is small, and the within-estimator is therefore inconsistent– consists of differencing the original equation, thus eliminating any (constant) individual effects. One can then use instrumental variables to estimate the parameters of the transformed equation. The use of instruments is necessary because of the induced serial correlation in the error term and the presence of lagged dependent variables. Such an estimation strategy has been first applied to a vector autoregressive model by Holtz-Eakin et al. (1988). Since our original data are in first differences (rates of growth), differencing them again would mean dealing with second differences, thus leading to all sorts of problems induced by overdifferencing. On the other hand, we have as many as twenty-seven observations –quite a large number for panel data. Because of this we have opted to use the dummy variables least squares estimator. In any case, we also estimated the model with instrumental variables and second differences. The results are very similar to the ones obtained with the dummy variables least square estimator, and for some sectors more favorable to our hypothesis.

Before discussing our results, it is worth pointing out the direction of our investigation. Because of adjustment costs and effort variations, cycles do affect contemporaneously measured productivity growth –i.e. , the Solow residual– regardless of the presence of externalities. It is difficult, therefore, to disentangle external effects within a static analysis. A dynamic analysis, on the other hand, can offer some insights.

Let us consider effort variations. After an increase in aggregate demand, in the presence of adjustment costs, effort is likely to increase in the short-run, in order to accommodate the increased demand. This would show up as an increase in the SR. In the medium run, however, effort would decrease and the labor force (and capital) would adjust to the new production levels. If this is indeed the case, the decrease in effort would result in a negative SR for one or more periods after the initial shock (unless effort variation effects are more than offset by "true" external effects).

Consider now thick market effects and other productive externalities, such as learning and knowledge spillovers. If they occur, a persistent increase in demand should have a persistent positive effect on the productivity level. In addition, if such an effect takes place, it could not be attributed to effort variations, since they clearly cancel out in the medium run. Therefore, we interpret a long-run increase in the productivity level above its starting value –following a persistent increase in aggregate output– as evidence of external effects.[5]

4.3 Empirical Results

We first estimated our model by pooling the four-digit industries (i) all together, and (ii) in two groups, namely durable and non-durable goods industries.

To take account of individual fixed-effects at the four-digit level, we used the familiar dummy variables least squares estimator, with two dummies for each industry: one for the pre-1973 period and one for post-1973. By so doing we try to capture a possible change in the trend of the variables after the oil crisis.[6] The SRs are derived using four types of inputs, i.e. production workers, non-productions workers, materials and capital.

For the purpose of our analysis, we analyze the path of the variables in the model after an aggregate shock. Our results are presented in the appendices of the chapter. As it can be seen in Table 4.1, innovations in aggregate output are highly persistent. That is, aggregate disturbances have a significant permanent effect on the level of aggregate activity. Having established this, we focus on the response of the sectoral productivity level (i.e., cumulated Solow residuals) to aggregate innovations.[7] The impulse responses are shown for the three models with, respectively, (i) durable goods industries, (ii) non-durable goods industries and (iii) all industries in Figures 4.1 to 4.3. The graphs trace the response of each variable to a unit (one standard error) orthogonal shock. All responses are measured as percent changes with respect to the equilibrium path. One standard error bands surround the point estimates of the responses.[8]

The following robust results emerge clearly from these graphs. First, innovations in aggregate output have a large contemporaneous positive effect on productivity. In the pooled model, for example, productivity increases in the same period by 2 percent in response to a unit standard error aggregate shock (an approximate size of 6 percent). This implies that theories which try to explain such an effect (such as those based on labor hoarding and effort variations or productive externalities) are worth pursuing.

Second, for the pooled model and the non-durables model productivity typically decreases for one or more periods following an aggregate shock, after an initial surge. We interpret such a result as evidence of effort variations. This sheds some light on some of the factors which may underlie the positive contemporaneous effect of aggregate demand on productivity. For the durables model, however, the level of productivity remains virtually unchanged after the initial increase. This suggests that either labor hoarding effects are not very important in these sectors, or, more likely, that the impact of effort variation on measured productivity is offset by that of "true" externalities.

Third, and perhaps more importantly, as time passes –after a persistent innovation in aggregate output– the productivity level does not return to its original level, but rather converges to a new, higher equilibrium level. In other words, there appears to be a permanent positive effect of aggregate activity on productivity. This result is much clearer for durables than for non-durables, although in both cases the t-test strongly rejects the null hypothesis of zero long-run response. The estimates of the long-run responses of the productivity level are reported in Table 4.2, together with the impact responses, for each model.

In order to get further empirical evidence, we estimated the model separately for each two-digit sector, by pooling four-digit industries within each of them. That is, we exploited the cross-section dimension of our sample to estimate separate VAR models for each two-digit industry. The fairly reasonable homogeneity among the cross-section units involved in such regressions would yield quite accurate estimates.

The estimates of both first-period and long-run responses of the level of productivity to aggregate shocks are reported, for each two-digit sector, in Table 4.3. It is worth pointing out that the new findings –although they vary widely across sectors– confirm all the main results observed with the more aggregate models. Also, at first sight, durable goods industries tend to show a larger long-run response of the productivity level to aggregate shocks than non-durable goods industries.

More formally, the significance of the long-run response of productivity can be assessed separately for each industry. We would reject the null hypothesis (zero long-run response) in 12 industries out of 19, at the 5% one-tail significance level. However, by doing so, the overall probability of rejecting a true null hypothesis increases with the number of industries, and is higher than the significance level for each industry. To avoid this, we use the sequential Bonferroni approach suggested by Holm (1979), and test the null hypothesis for each industry with an *overall* significance level α of 5%. That is, we consider the industry with the highest t-statistics –i.e., industry 35 (Machinery)– and set the significance level equal to α/n, where n is the number of industries. Notice that $\alpha/n = 0.0025$, which is significantly smaller than the original 0.05. Since the one-tail p-value corresponding to 15.6 (the t value of Machinery) is lower than 0.0025, we reject the null hypothesis with regard to industry 35. The sequential Bonferroni procedure requires that we examine the industry with the second-highest t-statistic, set the significance level equal to α/(n-1), perform the test, and so on, until we are unable to reject the null hypothesis. Such a procedure allows us to perform each test with the desired overall significance level. In our case, the procedure stopped at the 13th step, since we were unable to reject the null hypothesis for the 13th industry considered, i.e. Tobacco. There are 12 out of 19 sectors with significative long-run response, and these are starred in the table. They are mainly durable goods industries. This is consistent with the results obtained with the pooled models.

In Table 4.4 we present the forecast error variance decompositions for each of the three large VARs. Most of aggregate output is explained by the aggregate shock, a result that seems natural. Also a large part of the SR is explained by the sectoral shock, although not all of it. This result does not strongly support our hypothesis, since we are trying to insist on the influence of aggregate activity on sectoral productivity measures. However, a likely explanation of this phenomenon is the low correlation of very disaggregated data with a very aggregated variable (total manufacturing activity growth). The significance of the long-run responses of productivity to output are not casted into doubt by these variance decompositions.[9]

To test whether our results are affected by the aggregation level or any other feature of the data, we estimated the model using Jorgenson et al.'s (1987) data on two-digit industries. Again, we estimated three different models, by pooling respectively all industries, durable goods industries, and non-durable goods industries. The first-period and long-run response of the productivity level to innovations in aggregate output are reported in Table 4.5, for each model. The graphs of the impulse responses can be found in Figures 4.4–4.6.

The evidence available from this dataset largely confirms our main results. That is, aggregate innovations have a significant contemporaneous positive effect on sectoral productivity growth, and this effect becomes negative in the few periods which follow the shock, producing a decline in the level of productivity after the first period. More interestingly, the long-run response of the level of productivity is positive in all three models –although lower than that obtained with four-digit data– and statistically different from zero in both the pooled model and durable goods industries.

Our results are quite different from those obtained by Galí and Hammour (1993) and Saint-Paul (1993). They find that the long-run response of productivity to demand-induced economic expansions is negative. Our impulse responses indicate that it is either positive and significant or close to zero, depending on the industry. The difference in the findings is, in our opinion, most probably due to the way the respective models are identified. Galí and Hammour and Saint-Paul identify demand-induced expansions as those which have no contemporaneous effect on productivity. That is, they assume away external effects, one of the main channels through which demand might positively affect endogenous productivity. Moreover, their identification strictly requires the use of productivity measures adjusted for effort variations. As mentioned above, the derivation of such measures is to some extent arbitrary. Ultimately, therefore, the robustness of Galí and Hammour and Saint-Paul's results hinges upon the validity of both (i) their identification assumption and (ii) the adjustment of productivity measures.[10] We do not wish to deny the role played during recessions by productivity-improving activities, as described by Galí and Hammour and Saint-Paul, or the cleansing effects of slumps on techniques and enterprises, as emphasized long ago by Schumpeter (1939) and recently by Caballero and Hammour (1994). Rather, we interpret our results–along the lines of Galí and Hammour's theoretical model– as suggesting that the positive effects of expansions on productivity more than offset the negative ones.

Finally, one might suspect that our results are simply due to aggregate supply shocks, such as the 1973 and 1978 oil price shocks. This would also explain the difference between our results and those just mentioned. To investigate this point, we estimated an extended version of our VAR model, with three variables –the rate of growth of the oil price, the rate of growth of aggregate manufacturing output, and the sectoral SR. We achieved identification by imposing a Wold causal chain on the variables: the first variable is oil prices, the second aggregate activity growth, and the third sectoral SR. In this way, we are assuming that oil prices are exogenous within the year, but that they may affect the level of activity and the sectoral SR.

With such a model we can disentangle oil price disturbances, and therefore can interpret aggregate shocks to manufacturing output as mainly demand shocks. Both first-period and long-run responses of the productivity level to such aggregate disturbances are reported in Table 4.6, for the three pooled models, and 4.8 for each two-digit industry. As can be seen, the overall effect of aggregate activity on productivity has not diminished, and the long-run response is significantly different from zero in 8 out of 19 industries (starred in the table) at the 5% overall significance level, using to the sequential Bonferroni procedure. We also estimated the extended model with the Jorgenson data (Table 4.7). Although the estimates of the response of productivity to aggregate shocks are smaller with these data than those obtained with four-digit data, they are still positive.

4.4 Conclusion

In recent years there has been a number of papers –both theoretical and empirical– investigating the existence of externalities which make the output of one firm, or one industry, complementary to the output of other firms or industries, or to the aggregate economic activity, at business cycle frequencies. Most spillovers are usually assumed to be on the demand side, as in the models by Kiyotaki (1988) and Murphy et al. (1989). However, a number of studies in both fields of business cycle analysis and growth theory have emphasized the role of high-frequency productive externalities.

The first empirical evidence of external effects is due to Caballero and Lyons (1990 and 1992) and Bartelsman, Caballero and Lyons (1994). Our analysis differs from theirs in that we adopt a dynamic approach. This allows us to disentangle externalities from effort variation effects without using proxies for effort. Our results suggest the existence of labor hoarding in US manufacturing industry (which we will analyze in depth in the next chapter). More interestingly, we find evidence of external effects. These external effects point to the potential presence of aggregate increasing returns and multiple equilibria. Finally, unlike recent papers by Galí and Hammour (1993) and Saint-Paul (1993), we find no evidence of long-run negative effects of expansions on productivity.

Notes

[1]See Pelloni (1997) for an extension to the case of imperfect competition.

[2]The two approaches are very close to each other, since the adjusted productivity measures are obtained by regressing unadjusted data against proxies for effort.

[3]For simplicity, we omit the vector of means from the representation.

[4]Note that the disturbances $e(t)$ are mutually uncorrelated by construction. See for example Luetkepohl (1991). Note also that P is not uniquely defined, up to this point.

[5]Since aggregate activity affects sectoral productivity, internal increasing returns are not likely to be the only explanation of our findings. Another interpretation would be based on common technology shocks. We do not explore this possibility here. On technological shocks and procyclical productivity, see Prescott (1986) and Bernanke and Parkinson (1991).

[6]See Perron (1989).

[7]We calculate the response of the SR to aggregate shocks and then cumulate these increases to a given initial level, in order to obtain the response of the productivity level.

[8]Standard errors are computed from the asymptotic distribution of the response estimates given by Luetkepohl (1991).

[9]The variance decompositions for the two-digit results can be found in Chapter 5. There we calculate as well the standard deviations of the historical decompositions and Granger causality tests.

[10]Another reason for the different results may lie in the aggregation level of the data used, since Galí and Hammour and Saint-Paul use economy-wide data, and the aggregation levels of ΔY and Δs are the same in their model.

Appendix 1: Tables of Results.

Table 4.1: *Response of aggregate output level to aggregate shocks (percent).*

	First Period		Long Run	
	Response	s.e.	Response	s.e.
Pooled model	5.56	0.04	6.49	0.09
Durables	5.55	0.06	6.54	0.14
Non-durables	5.57	0.05	6.51	0.11

Note: Annual data for four-digit SIC manufacturing industries. The coefficients of the VAR(1) are estimated using two dummies for each industry (pre and post-1973). The asymptotic standard errors of the impulse responses are estimated following Luetkepohl (1991).

Table 4.2: *Response of productivity level to aggregate shocks (percent).*

	First Period		Long Run	
	Response	s.e.	Response	s.e.
Pooled model	2.06	0.06	1.88	0.09
Durables	2.41	0.07	2.42	0.11
Non-durables	1.47	0.10	0.97	0.15

Note: Annual data for four-digit SIC manufacturing industries. The coefficients of the VAR(1) are estimated using two dummies for each industry (pre and post-1973). The asympotic standard errors of the impulse responses are estimated following Luetkepohl (1991).

Table 4.3: *Response of productivity level to aggregate shocks (percent). Two digit industries.*

	First Period		Long Run	
	Response	s.e.	Response	s.e.
21. Tobacco	0.92	0.60	1.03	0.87
22. Textile mill	1.08	0.24	0.02	0.35
23. Apparel	0.95	0.22	0.39	0.30
24. Lumber-Wood	0.30	0.29	-1.36	0.38
25. Furniture	2.51	0.28	1.85*	0.41
26. Paper	1.67	0.23	1.09*	0.33
27. Printing	1.60	0.24	1.45*	0.34
28. Chemicals	2.91	0.26	2.89*	0.41
29. Petroleum-Coal	1.09	0.57	0.89	0.98
30. Rubber-Plastic	2.38	0.40	2.35*	0.55
31. Leather	-0.19	0.39	-0.96	0.54
32. Stone-Clay-Glass	2.28	0.20	1.98*	0.29
33. Primary Metals	2.63	0.28	2.36*	0.38
34. Fabr. Metals	2.66	0.18	2.47*	0.27
35. Machinery	2.96	0.17	4.36*	0.26
36. Electric Mach.	3.10	0.18	3.13*	0.30
37. Transportation Eqm.	1.57	0.27	1.31*	0.40
38. Instruments	1.80	0.28	2.53*	0.40
39. Miscellaneous	2.29	0.31	1.57*	0.43

Note: Annual data for four-digit SIC manufacturing industries. The coefficients of the VAR(1) are estimated using two dummies for each industry (pre and post-1973). The starred long-run responses are those significant at 5 percent level according to the Bonferroni sequential procedure described in the text.

Table 4.4: *Variance decomposition of the SR model. Percentage of forecast error explained by the sectoral shock.*

	First Period		Long Run	
	Y	SR	Y	SR
Pooled model	0	90	10	99
Durables	0	99	14	99
Non-durables	0	95	6	99

Note: Columns tagged 'Y' contain the percentage of the forecast error variance decomposition of aggregate output explained by the sectoral shock. Columns under 'SR' refer to the part of the SR explained by the sectoral shock. The first-period sectoral component of aggregate output is imposed by the identifying assumption.

Table 4.5: *Response of productivity level to aggregate shocks with Jorgenson's two-digit data (percent).*

	First Period		Long Run	
	Response	s.e.	Response	s.e.
Pooled model	0.85	0.11	0.44	0.20
Durables	1.11	0.15	0.67	0.31
Non-durables	0.55	0.15	0.16	0.24

Note: Annual data for two-digit SIC manufacturing industries. The coefficients of the VAR(1) are estimated using two dummies for each industry (pre and post-1973).

Table 4.6: *Response of productivity level to aggregate shocks in the 3-variables VAR (percent).*

	First Period		Long Run	
	Response	s.e.	Response	s.e.
Pooled model	2.05	0.06	1.95	0.09
Durables	2.46	0.07	2.48	0.11
Non-durables	1.38	0.10	1.06	0.15

Note: Annual data for four-digit SIC manufacturing industries. The coefficients of the VAR(1) are estimated using two dummies for each industry (pre and post-1973). The other responses of the VAR are omitted here.

Table 4.7: *Response of productivity level to aggregate shocks in the 3-variables VAR with Jorgenson's data (percent).*

	First Period		Long Run	
	Response	s.e.	Response	s.e.
Pooled model	0.44	0.10	0.08	0.15
Durables	0.57	0.15	0.09	0.23
Non-durables	0.30	0.15	0.03	0.18

Note: Annual data for two-digit SIC manufacturing industries. The coefficients of the VAR(1) are estimated using two dummies for each industry (pre and post-1973). The other responses of the VAR are omitted here.

Table 4.8: *Response of productivity level to aggregate shocks in the 3-variables VAR (percent). Two-digit industries.*

Industry	First Period		Long Run	
	Response	s.e.	Response	s.e.
21. Tobacco	0.21	0.58	-0.19	0.63
22. Textile mill	0.77	0.24	0.11	0.27
23. Apparel	0.78	0.22	0.33	0.23
24. Lumber-Wood	-0.08	0.29	-0.88	0.29
25. Furniture	1.81	0.27	0.94*	0.30
26. Paper	0.81	0.23	0.11	0.24
27. Printing	1.34	0.23	0.93*	0.26
28. Chemicals	1.54	0.25	0.62	0.29
29. Petroleum-Coal	0.88	0.57	0.67	0.73
30. Rubber-Plastic	1.63	0.39	0.89	0.41
31. Leather	0.02	0.39	-0.25	0.40
32. Stone-Clay-Glass	1.22	0.19	0.45	0.21
33. Primary Metals	1.71	0.27	0.91*	0.27
34. Fabr. Metals	1.52	0.17	0.68*	0.19
35. Machinery	2.15	0.16	1.96*	0.18
36. Electric Mach.	1.87	0.17	1.00*	0.20
37. Transportation Eqm.	0.89	0.26	0.34	0.30
38. Instruments	1.52	0.28	1.36*	0.28
39. Miscellaneous	1.71	0.31	0.95*	0.32

Note: Annual data for four-digit SIC manufacturing industries. The coefficients of the VAR(1) are estimated using two dummies for each industry (pre and post-1973). The other responses of the VAR are omitted here. The starred long run responses are those significant at 5 percent level according to the Bonferroni sequential procedure described in the text.

Appendix 2: Responses of Productivity Level to an Impulse in Aggregate Activity.

Figure 4.1: Durables

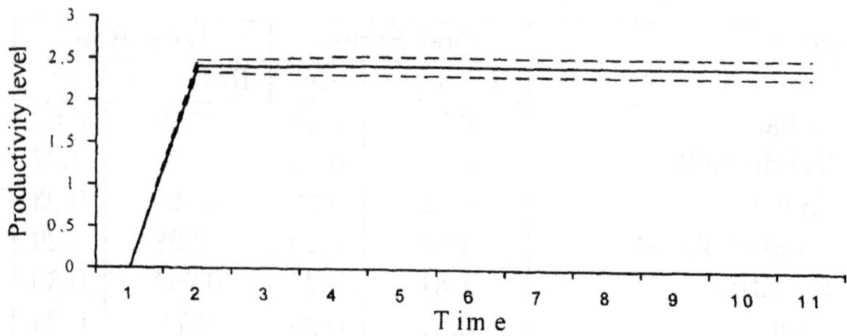

Figure 4.2: Non-Durables

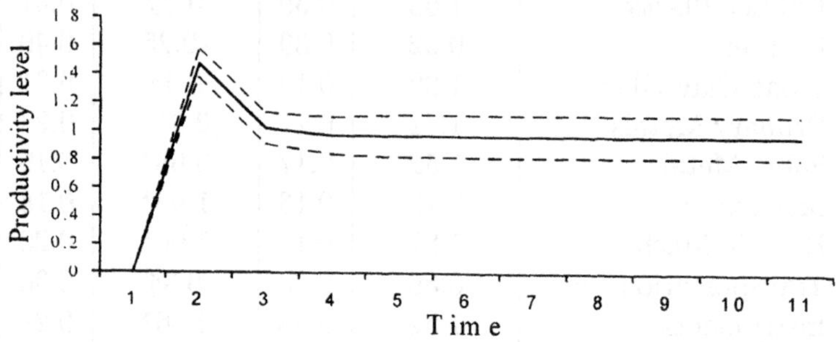

Figure 4.3: All industries

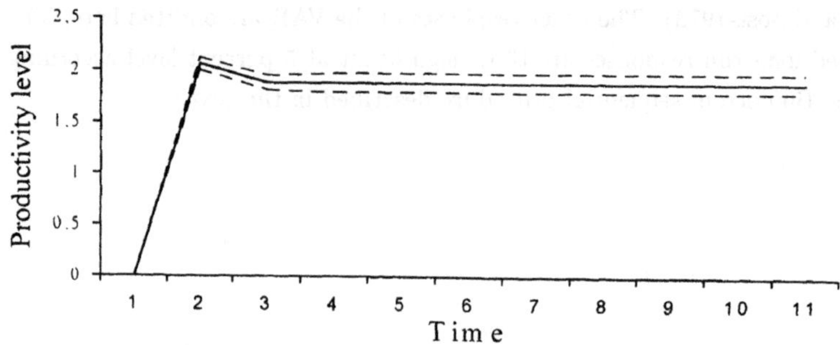

JORGENSON DATA: RESPONSES OF PRODUCTIVITY LEVEL TO AN IMPULSE IN AGGREGATE ACTIVITY.

Figure 4.4: Durables

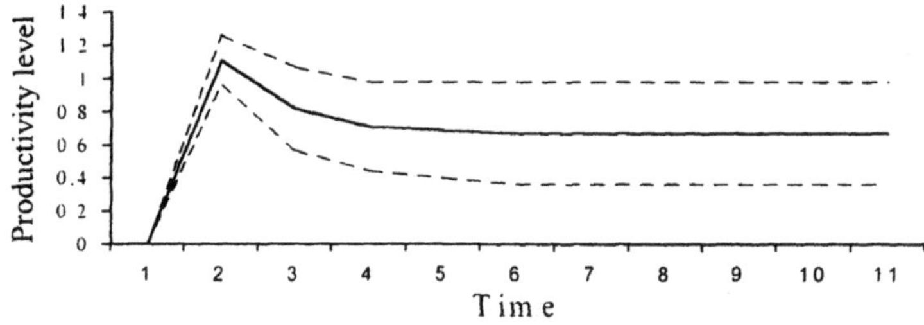

Figure 4.5: Non-Durables

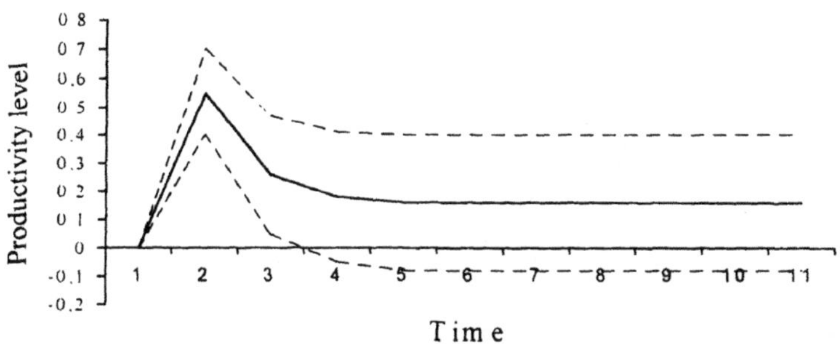

Figure 4.6: All industries.

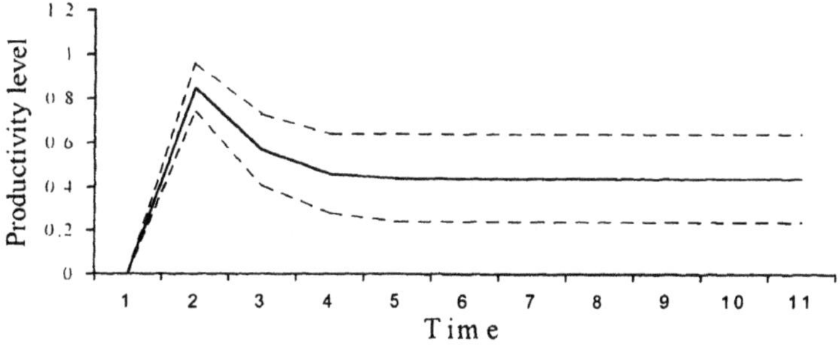

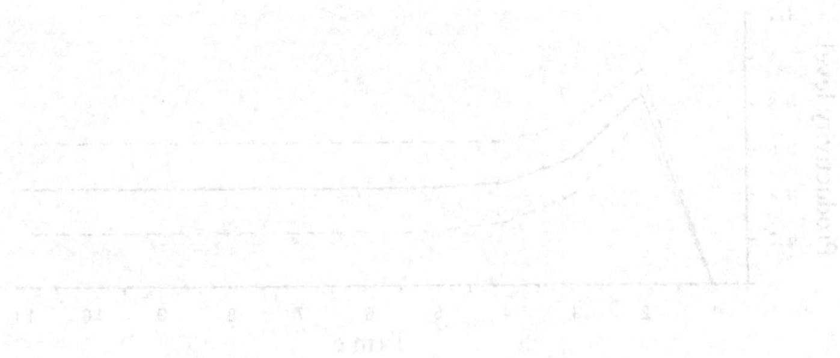

5

Labor Hoarding and Effort Variations

5.1 Introduction

In Chapter 3 and Chapter 4 we looked at two alternative hypotheses that have been suggested in the literature in order to explain the procyclical behavior of the SR. Both stress the role of demand as the main source of economic fluctuations, and in this sense challenge the emphasis put by RBC models on technology shocks.

In Chapter 3 we attributed the observed correlation of measured productivity and sectoral instruments of demand to the presence of markups. Firms price their output at a markup on their marginal cost. As a consequence, revenue shares of inputs do not capture the elasticities of the production function well, and are not the correct weights to use when calculating the contribution of factors of production to the change in output. Thus, there is a spurious element in the SR that does not reflect true changes in productivity, but rather cyclical movements of sectoral output driven by demand shocks.

In Chapter 4, instead, we interpreted the correlation between sectoral SRs and aggregate activity as evidence of external effects. Sectoral SRs respond positively to an aggregate shock because there is an increase in productivity which arises from technical complementarities or other kind of externalities. In this case it is assumed that the SR captures productivity changes well, i.e. it takes that part of the increase in output that is not explained by inputs' own changes but by this external effect. However, the comovement of the SR with aggregate activity is not taken as evidence of technology shocks, like in RBC models, but rather as a consequence of aggregate demand shocks. Externalities and markups are in some sense two alternative interpretations of the same phenomenon, i.e. the contemporaneous comovement of productivity measures and proxies of demand.

Of course when we interpret aggregate shocks mainly as demand shocks we are ruling out the possibility that aggregate impulses are produced by technology. Identifying "aggregate" with "demand" and "sectoral" with "technology" is very controversial, and we do not intend to settle this question here. The argument that demand shocks have a very important aggregate component is something obvious that does not have to be defended. The existence of a monetary or a tax policy tells us that they are powerful instruments that affect simultaneouly most branches of economic activity. But we do not intend to undervalue the theoretical importance of those models of economic fluctuations that stress the role of demand spillovers between small units and can thus produce large fluctuations in the whole of the economy after some lag.

On the other hand, the RBC literature does not clarify if technology shocks have an origin at an aggregate or disaggregate level. It does not pretend to do so, either. Long and Plosser's (1983) article tries to show how small independent shocks can coordinate and add up to an aggregate wave in technology, but of course this does not rule out the possibility of technology changes that affect many sectors of the economy at the same time. The computer industry is the classical case. New managerial techniques that may be applied to a wide range of industries are another example. In any case, we still believe that we can broadly identify shocks to aggregate activity with demand and shocks to sectoral productivity measures with technology. We do not give any new evidence on the matter and recognize that part of the interpretation of our results (the ones that assign the source of externalities to demand, and the one that relates markups to demand shocks) follows from this assumption. But the other part of our results, i.e. the long-run effect of "aggregate activity" (not demand) on various sectoral variables, does not depend on the assumption of sector specific technology shocks. Needless to say, benchmark articles on these subjects like Hall (1988) and Caballero and Lyons (1992) use implicitly the same assumptions as we do without discussing them.

Our identification assumption also relies on the size of the sectors used. Not only we rule out the possibility of aggregate technology, but also we assume that sectoral technology shocks do not add up to a contemporaneous effect on the aggregate, which could be casted into doubt with our yearly data. However, the low level of aggregation of the sectors of the panel suggest that this effect is not likely to be very important.

In both chapters we have noted that there can be a problem in the measurement of the effective labor input due to the fact that labor takes time to adjust to permanent shocks to demand. When we estimate markups (in a static model) the slow adjustment of labor produces a bias, whereas in the VAR model of externalities the bias is produced only in the immediate response and disappears in the long run.

Here we look at two different types of biases in the measurement of productivity growth considered in the literature, namely, labor hoarding and effort variations.[1] These concepts are not clearly defined in many studies on the matter, and sometimes they correspond to slightly different things depending on the author. Labor hoarding does not necessarily imply a reduction in effort, because hoarded workers may be put to work in activities not recorded as final output (like repairing machines, painting buildings, re-training). Similarly, changes in effort may be the result of making employees work overtime, with or without being paid, or may be a genuine improvement in "effort" in periods of very high demand, producing more with the same hours worked (which is in practical terms a temporary increase in productivity, although not the result of an improvement in technology). In none of these cases we can talk of labor hoarding, strictly speaking.

Independently of what exact definition of both terms we are using, what matters to us in the first place is that in both cases there will be a bias in the SR, and also one of the same amount in the DSR if the implied remuneration of unmeasured labor shows up immediately in the data, that is, if measured wages move together with effective labor. Wages are usually calculated as the ratio of remuneration over the quantity of labor:

$$W = \frac{WN}{N} \tag{5.1}$$

thus there will be a change in W when we measure remuneration WN correctly but the quantity of labor N incorrectly (because labor hoarding or changes in effort). This spurius change in wages is reflected in the DSR. Otherwise, if the pay of unmeasured labor is not reflected in the data (such that WN does not change), the bias on the SR will be different that the one on the DSR.

In any case, whatever the relationship in the short run between the biases on the SR and on the DSR, the effect of these biases will disappear in the long run, such that the long-run effect of aggregate activity on the SR and the DSR given by a VAR model should be the same. The reason for this is that measured labor and wages should move towards the new levels of effective labor and wages when the costs of adjustment disappear. This is the second point we make in this chapter.

Let us consider first the effects of labor hoarding and effort variations on the SR. If there are adjustment costs to labor, some firms may hoard employees in the face of a recession, instead of laying them off, for fear of losing the specific training given to them. When there is a permanent drop in demand, they will adjust the quantity of labor to the new situation only after some lag, once they realize that the level of demand will not rise to the starting point. A spurious negative SR produced by the initial shock would be counteracted by positive SRs in subsequent periods because the firm will reduce the quantity of measured labor while adapting to the new level of demand. Hence the *level* of measured productivity is negative in the first period and goes back to the original point after some time, producing the pattern of response that we identified as effort changes in the previous chapter.

However, Hall (1988) has demonstrated that labor hoarding is not enough to produce a spurious procyclical residual, because of movements of the labor share. This point was already explained in Chapter 3. Here we will argue that labor hoarding is likely to be accompanied by countercyclical markups to avoid losses (by maintining prices rigid at the level of the average cost, and therefore producing a stable labor share), and in this case the estimation of the markup from the SR equation will in fact be biased.

Strictly speaking, "hoarding labor" means retaining workers in the firm, and this would be done only in recessions. In a broader sense, we can consider that labor hoarding is a symmetric phenomenon, meaning that the number of workers in the firm fluctuates less than in would in the absence of adjustment costs.

Let us consider now effort changes. They are another type of labor mismeasurement that introduces a bias in the SR in the presence of costs of adjustement for labor. Firms may choose to raise the required effort per worker when demand goes up, instead of increasing the number of workers, because the cost of the latter option is higher. Even in the absence of costs of adjustment for labor, firms might be indifferent (if the costs of each alternative are equal) between changing the quantity of effective labor by increasing the number of workers or by raising the required effort per worker, and may choose the effort option temporarily until they are sure that the changes in demand are permanent. Unmeasured changes in effort also produce a spurious change in the SR, because there is a change in output produced by a change in effective labor input that is not reflected in measured labor.

Not surprisingly, labor hoarding and effort changes are treated very often as the same phenomenon.[2]

To summarize this issue, we will talk of a spurious SR produced by adjustment costs of labor when, in the absence of true variations in productivity, output changes and measured labor does not. As costs of adjustment disappear, the bias on the SR will vanish.

Let us look now at the effects of labor hoarding and effort changes on the DSR, assuming that there are not externalities or technology shocks. Here the main point is how effort changes are paid, because this issue will affect the way measured wages are computed. In principle, labor hoarding without effort variations should not influence measured wages. Labor hoarding with effort variations or effort changes on their own have an effect on measured wages and therefore on the DSR if effort is compensated in a period-by-period basis (as Roeger (1995) assumes), because WN will move and N will remain stable in equation 5.1. If effort is not compensated, or if it is compensated on a long-run basis (more effort in times of booms is paid with less effort in times of slumps), measured wages will remain constant and so will the DSR, because both WN and N will not change.

If effort variation is compensated on a period-by-period basis, the reaction of the DSR to a permanent positive shock in demand will be similar to that of the SR: a positive DSR in the initial period will be followed by negative values in subsequent periods, because the firm will substitute new workers for effort as it recognizes the permanent character of the shock. Therefore measured wages will go back to their initial level (a change of W in the opposite direction of the initial one in subsequent periods).

The response of the DSR in a VAR model like the one in Chapter 4 will be parallel to that of the SR. Similarly, the bias that effort variations induce in the estimation of the markup in Chapter 3 will be the same in the SR and in the DSR equations. Again, we are considering that results in Chapter 3 are a mirror image to those in Chapter 4, in the sense that markups and externalities explain the same basic correlation.

In this chapter a VAR model similar to that in Chapter 4 is applied. There we developed explicitly a dynamic framework to try to identify the degree of effort changes. We attributed the contemporaneous correlation of sectoral SRs and aggregate demand to externalities, while recognizing that effort changes can bias that relationship. In the VAR model this bias disappears in the long run, leaving just that part of measured productivity that corresponds to true externalities. In the following sections we are going to exploit the properties of a VAR that combines sectoral variables with aggregate activity and apply the same principle to other variables –those that take time to adjust will have a temporary low response to the aggregate shock, and this will show up the long run. In this way we look for some complementary evidence on the existence of some degree of variation in labor utilization over the business cycle, while recognizing that the change in labor utilization may be produced not only by effort changes, but also by labor hoarding.

Specifically, we look at two extensions of our previous work. First, we apply the VAR model of Chapter 4 to the DSR. A permanent aggregate shock will have an immediate effect on the dual measure of productivity that can be explained either by external effects or by imperfect competition, following the conclusions of the third and the fourth chapters. This basic relationship can be modified by the effect of effort changes, as we have argued, if effort is compensated on a current basis and this produces a bias in measured wages and thus in the DSR. Labor hoarding might also bias that relationship through a change in output prices (not through salaries), but we do not think that this effect is quantitatively important. This would be the case if labor hoarding were together with a reduction in the output price because the firm is competitive and pushes prices down to the level of marginal cost, which is very low when firms hoard labor.

The bias due to immediately compensated effort variation will be negative in recessions because of a reduction in measured wages, which enter the DSR with a positive sign:

$$DSR = \alpha(w - p) + \beta(v - p) + (1 - \alpha - \beta)(y - k)$$

The second bias (the one of labor hoarding and a reduction in prices) will be positive in recessions, because the reduction in the price enters the DSR with a negative sign. This second case is less likely also because it implies temporary losses for the firm.

In either case, as time passes and the firm adapts its quantity of labor to the new level of demand, labor hoarding or effort changes are reversed. The effect on the DSR has a sign which is opposite to the one in the first period, and the net effect of the bias on the level of productivity (measured as cumulated DSRs) is zero. Productivity levels will move responding to the true degrees of externalities or markups. The logic of this dynamic response is analogous to the one of the SR when there are effort changes. As in that case, the difference between the long and the short-run responses can be attributed to temporary adjustments in labor or labor compensation.

As a second extension, we simulate the response of the level of sectoral output, labor and the use of materials to a shock in aggregate activity. This gives a more direct evidence of the degree of changing factor utilization embodied in the behavior of the SR. The idea is that the downward movement in the level of productivity after the initial shock is not matched by a parallel movement in the sectoral employment level, but rather by a slow labor response. Permanent shocks to aggregate output permanently change the level of sectoral employment (and in practice they change it even more in subsequent periods, as we will see).

In all cases, the identifying restriction of the VAR models is the same as in Chapter 4. We assume that sectoral variables cannot significantly affect aggregate output. Rather, it is aggregate production, probably as a reflection of aggregate demand, what *causes* sectoral activity. Again, the identification of "aggregate" as "demand" can be subject to the criticisms already explained.

All the VAR models we use are bivariate and are estimated for each two-digit sectors with one dummy variable for each four-digit industry.

The next section revises other possible specification errors whose quantitative importance is dismissed by Hall and looks in more detail at the implications of labor hoarding and effort changes for the SR and the DSR, comparing the results of Chapter 4 with a similar VAR model with the DSR.

5.2 Specification Errors

5.2.1 *Hall's* Non-explanations

Hall (1988 and 1990) discusses very carefully those measurement errors that could possibly bias his results. His conclusion is that it is not likely that any specification errors explain the cyclical behavior of the SR. According to him markups are a key element in explaining the cyclical behavior of the SR. He suggests that increasing returns to scale or permanent excess capacity are probably important in explaining the co-existence of markups and the absence of large profits in US manufacturing. He investigates the importance of increasing returns in his 1990 contribution, where he estimates the degree of returns to scale using the SR calculated with cost shares instead of revenue shares. The results he obtained in his paper are difficult to believe (because of very large estimates of returns to scale), so his conclusions must be interpreted with caution. He admits that externalities are a plausible alternative to markups, and this is confirmed by Caballero and Lyons (1990), who apply his method to more disaggregated data and find that in fact increasing returns to scale are found only at highly aggregated levels of activity.

As pointed out by Hall (1990), among the hypotheses that cannot explain the correlation of the SR with demand (what he calls *non-explanations* of procylical SR) are those that produce a cyclical input share, but do not affect its mean. Examples of these may be wage smoothing, or rigid prices.[3] Provided these phenomena make the revenue share symmetric around the long-run average of the elasticity of output with respect to each input, they will not bias the correlation of the SR with the instruments. This is because a positive bias in times of recession will be exactly compensated by a negative one during expansions. Symmetry ensures that these biases cancel out.

Other misspecification errors could in theory bias the estimation of markups, but their magnitude is likely to be small. Among these Hall cites pure measurement errors in the number of hours. The error in the total number of hours is probably in the measurement of the number of hours per worker, rather than the number of workers. However, changes in the number of workers account for most of the variability of total hours. Measurement errors in the number of workers would have to be very large to explain the actual movements of the SR. Furthermore, Hall measures hours carefully combining different sources of data. Measurement errors in capital are dismissed by Hall using the same type of arguments; i.e. these errors should have to be implausibly large to account for the variability of measured productivity.

5.2.2 The Difference Between Labor Hoarding and Effort Variations

Once it is shown that these specification errors are not of enough magnitude to significantly bias the estimation of markups, labor hoarding remains for Hall as the main alternative explanation of procyclical productivity. He demonstrates that if labor hoarding (without effort variations) is to bias his method for estimating markups, it must be the case that the price charged by the firm exceeds its marginal cost by more than the normal markup.

His argument goes as follows. Labor hoarding implies that the marginal cost is temporarily very low, since production can be increased at almost no cost by putting "hoarded" employees to work (here he is assuming that their activity has no value). Imagine a situation in which labor is the only input. If the firm is competitive (or if it wants to maintain its normal markup), it will have to lower its price to the new level of MC and thus the markup will be larger than the ratio of price to average cost AC. The AC is given by the level of wages, which are supposed to be kept constant in the labor hoarding regime.

$$\frac{P}{MC} > \frac{P}{AC}$$

In this situation the price moves below average cost producing losses and inducing an increase in the labor share

$$\alpha = \frac{WN}{PQ}$$

The increase of α compensates the rigidity of recorded labor when output goes down in a recession. In the example given by Hall (1988) these two changes exactly cancel out. In a strict competitive situation (where price follows marginal cost even if this is nearly zero) labor hoarding should not induce a spurius SR.

However, it would be a natural response in a non-competitive framework that the firm maintains the price at the level of AC during recessions, hence avoiding losses. The markup of price over marginal cost increases and the ratio of price over average cost remains constant. So do the labor share and the profit rate. The labor share being constant, labor hoarding produces a negative SR and therefore a spurious procyclical SR. That is, only if the markup is countercyclical (it is over its average level during recessions) can labor hoarding explain the behavior of the SR. This is why Hall argues that labor hoarding cannot on its own (without markups) explain the correlation of the SR with instruments of demand. What he does not say explicitly is that labor hoarding would also bias the estimation of the markup, because the markup is calculated as a fixed parameter, and is ill-suited to capture this special type of countercyclical behavior of margins. What is estimated is an *average* markup between the *normal* one and the one under the labor hoarding regime.

As an extension to Hall's work, and trying to capture the possible cyclical pattern of markups, Domowitz et al. (1988) include a regression with varying parameters, letting the markup vary with some indicator of the cycle. We have repeated this excercise with our data set but found only small effects of cycle indicators on the markups and these only in some sectors. These effects are not significantly different from zero, and the sign of the cyclical influence of the markup varies depending on the industry, so therefore results are inconclussive. In Chapter 3, Tables 3.22 and 3.23 we have seen that the corrected SR and DSR are not clearly correlated with GNP growth or the rate of growth of oil prices. All these results indicate that we have not been able to find the clear cyclical pattern of markups that Domowitz et al. found and that is claimed by some theories of the business cycle (Rotemberg and Woodford, 1991).

A different way of interpreting labor hoarding (and overhead labor) is to view them as examples of a short-run fixity of an input. They are treated by Morrison (1992) as temporary capacity underutilizations of labor. There is an excess capacity during recessions which is not taken into account, and which produces a movement of the SR parallel to output. Spare capacity implies that marginal cost is very low and firms have to price their output at the level of average cost if they want to avoid losses. Otherwise, the share of labor will go up and compensate the slow adjustment of labor. Alternatively, temporary capacity underutilization will be compensated by a temporary (and therefore countercyclical) markup. This view of labor hoarding as a change in capacity utilization is more in the line of a symmetric interpretation of labor hoarding: labor hoarding is also possible during expansions.

We have indicated above that labor hoarding can occur with or without effort variations. In the case of labor hoarding without effort variations the stability of output prices and of input shares means that a lower marginal cost is accomodated by a higher markup (producing countercyclical markups). When there are effort variations stable shares do not necessarily imply that markups move. The shares remain stable because the markup does not change. If effort is remunerated (be it on a long term agreement or on a current basis), firms will regard effort as part of their marginal cost. When a change in activity is tackled through a change in effort (instead of a change in the quantity of labor), the marginal cost remains constant, and so does the price of output. Of course we will not be able to discriminate between these differences by looking only at the SR.

However, the type of compensation of effort may be important because of its effects on computed wages, and therefore for the calculation of the DSR. As Roeger (1995) has shown, if effort changes are paid through an increase in current salaries, the computed wage will be positively correlated with effort. This in turn will produce a corresponding movement in the DSR. On the other hand, if more effort in expansions is compensated by less effort in recessions, with the wage set at the level of average marginal productivity, wages will not co-vary with effort and the DSR will not reflect effort changes. Roeger assumes in his paper that effort is compensated in a period-by-period basis, and therefore effort will move with measured wages. Under this assumption, the specification error that effort imposes on the SR is equal to the one on the DSR, such that the difference between them (the dependent variable in his estimating equation) is not affected by effort. However, instant remuneration of effort is only an assumption. A long-run agreement implies more stable wages and produces a DSR being less cyclical than the SR. In our VAR model, whatever the influence of changes of effort on the SR or the DSR in the short run, it should disappear after the economy adjusts to the new simulated level of activity.

To sum up, labor hoarding with or without effort variations produces a spurious SR if the labor share remains stable. In the case of labor hoarding without effort variations, a stable share results from rigid prices and a markup that rises above its normal level during recessions, such that a shifting price-to-marginal cost ratio compensates a shifting average cost-to-marginal cost ratio. In the case of labor hoarding with changes in effort, the share does not move because the marginal cost (and the markup) do not move. As to the effect on the DSR, labor hoarding (without effort variations) does not affect the DSR. Effort variations will affect recorded wages and the DSR if it is compensated on a current basis. The effect will be zero if it is compensated by long-run agreement. In either case, the effects of both specification errors on both residuals should vanish in the long run as variables adjust to their new long-run equilibrium.

5.2.3 Results and Interpretation

The results of the bivariate VAR that models aggregate output change and the DSR are presented in Table 5.4 in Appendix 1 and in the graphics of Appendix 2. The table gives the short and the long-run responses of the level of productivity (measured as cumulated DSRs) to a shock in aggregate output. The graphics show this response together with the corresponding results from the VAR of the SR, in Chapter 4, although here we have used SRs constructed with only one type of labor input, that is, without separating production workers from non-production workers. The reason is that we cannot obtain the growth rate of wages for both types of workers separately, and we prefer to define both the SR and the DSR for the same definition of labor, i.e. all workers. The results of the VAR model with the new definition of the SR can be found in Table 5.1.

As in Chapter 4, the VAR has been estimated by pooling sectors at four-digit SIC level within every two-digit manufacturing industry, and including four-digit sectoral dummy variables to account for idiosyncratic effects at the lowest level of aggregation. The bands show the one standard error confidence intervals of the impulse responses.

For most sectors the dynamic pattern of the SR and the DSR is similar. After an initial positive response, due to the contemporaneous correlation of measured productivity with aggregate output, the level of productivity remains stable or goes down. Only for three sectors (35 Machinery, 36 Electric Machinery and 38 Instruments) there is a further increase after the first period. Although sectors 20 Tobacco, 30 Rubber and Plastic, 32 Stone-Glass and 34 Fabricated Metals present a point estimate of the long-run response slightly larger than the short-run response, the difference between them is statistically insignificant. In all cases, the increase in the productivity level can be explained as technical complementarities that occur over a period lower than one year, or simply as learning by doing.

As a general result, we can say that the level of measured productivity remains stable or falls marginally for durables. For non-durables there is a clear decreasing pattern from an initial level (which is also lower for these sectors than for durables). This suggests that externalities are an important phenomenon in durables industries, whereas for non-durables the evidence of external returns is weaker and it is mixed with an significant degree of slow labor adjustment.

As argued previously, the long-run response of productivity should reveal the magnitude of the external effect. Four industries out of 19 have a negative long-run response of cumulated DSR (industries 22 Textile, 23 Apparel, 24 Lumber-Wood and 31 Leather). Three of these (22, 24 and 31) have also a negative response in the VAR with the SR. Of the remaining sectors, two of them (26 Paper and 28 Petroleum and Coal) have point estimates indistinguishable from zero. The rest give sinificantly positive long-run responses.

From a comparison of the VAR's including the SR and the DSR we can infer some evidence as to the relative mix of labor hoarding and effort variations. On the one hand, we can observe that the contemporaneous response of the SR is in general larger than that of the DSR. A similar result also appeared in Chapter 3, where the correlation of the residuals with demand was interpreted as a markup. There markup estimates were bigger in the SR equation than in the DSR regression. Labor hoarding without effort variations is one explanation of this result. Effort variations which are not compensated on a current basis are another. We have argued that both hypotheses bias the SR but not the DSR.

On the other hand, decreases in the level of productivity after the initial shock which are common to both the SR the DSR are evidence of substitution of the quantity of labor for effort variations compensated on a current basis, because we have argued that compensated effort affects the SR and the DSR in a similar way. Finally, the long-run response of both residuals should be the same, since all the temporary changes in factor utilization that explain the initial shock should disappear in the long run, and what remains is the true degree of externalities. (Alternatively, if we believe that the correlation of the residuals with aggregate activity is an indication of markups then what remains is evidence of markups after the estimation bias has disappear).

We obtain mixed evidence on the validity on our framework. For nine sectors out of nineteen (25, 27, 30, 31, 32, 34, 36, 37 and 39) the long-run response of the cumulated SR and the DSR to a shock in aggregate activity is almost identical, even if the initial response was different. For these sectors (mainly durables' industries), the model *works*, in the sense that we obtain the same level of externality or markups after the allegedly temporary problems with the measurement of labor have disappeared. These measurement errors are a combination of labor hoarding and effort variations, and we have no evidence that one dominates the other.

For the remaining sectors we do not have convergent paths of the two levels of measured productivity to a common level, but rather a parallel trajectory, in most cases with the cumulated SRs above the level of the cumulated DSRs at all lags. This reveals either the existence of some element that biases our results and that does not depend on the rate of utilization of the factors, or simply the fact that the one standard error bands are large enough to avoid any definitive conclusion as to the validity of the model. In effect, the size of the bands averages 0.4-0.5 percentage points for the long-run response of each residual. This means that we can reject the hypothesis of equal response in very few cases (only for sectors 26 and 33).

Our main purpose in running VAR models with aggregate variables and the SR and the DSR has been to look at the pattern presented by the impulse responses. We can also give some information as to the relative importance of the two types of shocks considered (aggregate and sectoral) on the variables of the VAR (aggregate activity change and SR or DSR). Table 5.2 presents the forecast error variance decompositions of each of to the two variables of the SR VARs. For every two-digit VAR we have calculated up to ten period ahead decompositions. These give the percentage of the forecast error variance that is given by each of the individual shocks. To summarize information, we only provide the variance decompositions at 1 and 10 years, since there is almost no time evolution in the pattern of the results. In the first two columns we can find the contribution of the sectoral shock to the variance of the two variables in the model, respectively aggregate activity growth and the SR. The contribution of the aggregate shock to both variables is given by 100% minus the values in the first two columns. As it would be expected, the sectoral shock explains most of the SR, whereas the aggregate shock accounts for most of the variance of aggregate activity. This pattern is repeated at all lags. The very small values we find for the contribution of the sectoral shock to output means that the effect of sectoral technology shocks is almost zero. Here we must recall that we have ruled out aggregate technology shocks in our identification assumption. It seems natural that what we call "technology" at a very disaggregated level does not influence what we call "demand" at the economy level.

The contribution of the aggregate shock to sectoral productivity is not very large either, which is a relative surprise, since our main arguments try to stress the role of aggregate demand in driving the SR through externalities, markups or biases in the measurement of the effective quantity of labor. However, this effect is not negligible for some sectors, for which it arrives to values between 15% and 20% of the variance of the SR (industries 30, 32, 34, 35 and 36). In any case, a possible explanation of this relatively poor result lies in the different levels of aggregation of the data.

In Table 5.5 we present the forescast error variance decomposition for the DSR VAR. The results are very similar to those of the SR equation and no further comment is required.

As a final checking of the models we compute the value of an F-test for the null hypothesis of Granger non-causality of the aggregate shock on the sectoral SRs (and DSRs) and of the sectoral shock on aggregate activity. These are presented in Tables 5.3 and 5.6. The 5% critical value of the F-distribution with 1 degree of freedom in the numerator (the number of restrictions of the null, which is equal to the order of the VAR) and a variable number of degrees of freedom in the denominator (between 100 and infinite, in practical terms) is between 3.81 and 3.95. We cannot reject the hypothesis of Granger non-causality for a majority of sectors, although for others the rejection is very clear. The values of the test are higher for the influence of the aggregate shock on the sectoral variables. These results do not reinforce our hypothesis of an important aggregate component explaining the behavior of the SR and the DSR. However, we can maintain our conclusions, which are not rejected by the test (we take non-causality as the null), since they are supported by the values of the impulse responses which are statictically different from zero in many industries.

To summarize the results, the VAR model with the DSR confirms the results obtained in Chapter 4, and suggests that part of the initial response of the level of productivity is a combination of effort variations and labor hoarding. In addition, the responses of integrated SRs and DSRs converge in the long run to a common level for about half of our industries, revealing that once measurement errors are eliminated from both residuals what remains is a good indicator of externalities (or markups). Variance decompositions and Granger non-causality tests do not support strongly the importance of the aggregate shocks on productivity, although this can be partly explained by the use of a panel data with very different levels of aggregation in the variables.

It is not easy to disentangle what part of the long-run effect of demand shocks on the level of productivity is due to markups and what part is the result of external effects. We can use the estimates of markups in Chapter 3 to correct the shares of inputs and then create new series of productivity growth, a corrected SR (SRc) and a corrected DSR (DSRc), which would measure true productivity changes after we eliminate the effects of markups. To do so, we can apply the VAR model with aggregate activity to the SRc and the DSRc and check for any positive long-run effect on the level of productivity.

However, the results of this exercise (which we have omitted here) do not provide a satisfactory solution to the identification of markups separately from externalities. The impulse responses of the SRc and the DSRc are roughly parallel to those of the SR and the DSR, but starting from an initial point (the contemporaneous response) lower than in the case of these, and moving down to a final level which is underneath the original one.[4] The reason for this pattern is clear: The contemporaneous correlation of demand with the SR and the DSR can be attributed to both markups of externalities. Correcting both measures with the estimates of markups calculated in Chapter 3 means that we attribute all the correlation to the markup, leaving no room for the external effect. The effects of the slow adjustment of labor also appear with the SRc and the DSRc (since they are a shifted version of the SR and the DSR), and will result in a negative response in the long run. But they do not answer our question, i.e. what produces the correlation of demand instruments with productivity measures, markups or externalities.

5.3 The Response of Output, Labor and Materials to an Aggregate Shock

Up to this point we have found that the sectoral level of measured productivity rises and then decreases after a shock to aggregate activity. We have interpreted this decrease to a new long-run level as the effect of slow adjustment of labor and labor compensation. To confirm these results we extend here the VAR to induce the growth rates of sectoral output, labor and materials in order to observe directly the responses of real variables to an initial shock to aggregate activity.

The VAR estimation method is similar to the one used in the previous section. The identification of the VAR is also the same as before. In this case the justification for this criterion is not the lack of contemporaneous effect of sectoral SR on aggregate demand, but rather the fact that the sectors are very small. Of course that sectoral output or labor growth might affect aggregate activity (a simple accountancy principle would explain this). It is the fact of having four-digit variables vs. the whole manufacturing sector that minimizes the effect of the former on the later.

We look at the response of the level of output and the quantity of labor and materials to a shock in aggregate output. The results are presented in Tables 5.7, 5.10 and 5.13 in Appendix 1 and graphed in Appendix 2. All the three responses for each sector are included in the same graph, although for the sake of clarity we omit the one standard error bands.

For all sectors, except sector 22 Textiles, the long-run response of the labor input is larger than the contemporaneous response. This behavior is more apparent in the large durables' sectors (32-39), where only about half of the total long-run reaction of sectoral labor is recorded in the first period, and where the final level is also higher than in the other sectors. On the contrary, the response of sectoral output to the aggregate shock is much faster. For most sectors the final level of output is close to the response recorded in the first period. For some of them (industries 22 Textiles, 23 Apparel, 24 Lumber-Wood and 31 Leather) the long-run response is at a lower level than the short-run response. In almost all cases the contemporaneous level of output is within the two standard errors limits of the final level which means that we cannot reject the hypothesis that the level of output is stable one period after the initial shock for many sectors. Only sectors 33 Primary Metals, 34 Fabricated Metals and 35 Machinery show a further increase in output in subsequent periods, which can be understood as a multiplier effect of the initial shock. The behavior of materials is similar to that of output, but the response is not quite as fast. The adjustment in the utilization of the materials input after the initial impulse is not instantaneous, and continues in subsequent periods up to its final and high level.

We also present for these three models the variance decompositions and some Granger-causality tests. They can be found in Tables 5.8, 5.11, 5.14 for the variance decompositions, and 5.9, 5.12 and 5.15 for the Granger-causality tests. These results are very similar to those of the SR and the DSR VARs: the weak correlation of the aggregate and the sectoral variables make the models not being supported strongly by the data in the sense we look for. However, our main conclusions derive from the impulse responses.

We would only like to mention two characteristics that slightly differentiate the variance decompositions from the ones of the SR and the DSR. First, the percentage of the forecast error variance of sectoral output growth explained by the aggregate variable is larger than for other variables. This probably derives from reverse causation from sectoral to aggregate output. Second, the variance decomposition of labor after ten periods shows a larger effect of aggregate activity than the contemporaneous one. In this case the slow adjustment of labor to the shock is again the explanation. It gives new evidence of the bias produced by changes in effort.

5.4 Conclusion

The picture we obtain from these patterns is clear and confirms previous conclusions. The SR is correlated with aggregate activity, and a possible interpretation of this comovement is that aggregate output spurs the long-run level of productivity through external returns to scale. However, part of the contemporanous correlation of the SR with aggregate output growth is due to slow adjustment of labor or materials use. In Section 5.2.3 we interpret the downward movement of the SR after the shock as the result of this slow adjustment. In Section 5.3 we have presented more evidence on this issue. Of the main variables that determine the response of the SR, sectoral output change has an immediate response, whereas materials and especially labor adjust more slowly. Labor hoarding and effort variations seem to play an important role in the behavior of the SR over the cycle.

The importance of variations in labor utilization must not hide the main conclusions we reached in the previous two chapters. The adjustment of labor plays some role in explaining procyclical SR, but its magnitude is not large as compared to the high correlations we found there between sectoral measures of productivity and proxies of demand, especially in those (mainly durables) sectors which support more clearly our results.

However, taken together, Chapters 4 are 5 leave an open question. It is true that the SR and the DSR are procyclical, and it also appears to be true that this procyclicality is mainly due to demand-driven fluctuations, as we have tried to argue throughout this book. But the two interpretations of the correlation of productivity with demand are two alternative views of the same phenomenon, namely markups or external effects. The long-run level of productivity we have obtained in our VAR simulations can be taken as an indication of either. We still do not know to what extent one is more important than the other.

Notes

[1]Errors in the measurement of hours are not likely to be very large, as argued by Hall (1988), and discussed later.

[2]See, for example, Sbordone (1997) and Caballero and Lyons (1992).

[3]In both cases there is an implicit equilibrium in the equality of observed wage to long-run marginal productivity of labor or of the rigid price to the long-run marginal cost.

[4]This result is equivalent to the lack of correlation of the SRc and the DSRc with real GNP growth and oil price growth, shown in Chapter 3.

APPENDIX 1: TABLES OF RESULTS

Table 5.1: *VAR of aggregate output growth and SR. Response of productivity level to aggregate output (percent).*

	First period		Long run	
	Response	s.e.	Response	s.e.
21. Tobacco	0.83	0.62	1.05	0.89
22. Textile Mill	0.99	0.27	-0.21	0.43
23. Apparel	0.96	0.24	0.18	0.38
24. Lumber-Wood	0.03	0.32	-1.60	0.43
25. Furniture	2.56	0.38	1.87	0.55
26. Paper	1.55	0.25	0.97	0.36
27. Printing	1.56	0.24	1.27	0.37
28. Chemicals	2.74	0.28	2.77	0.45
29. Petroleum-Coal	0.72	0.61	0.84	1.07
30. Rubber-Plastic	2.24	0.40	2.25	0.54
31. Leather	-0.26	0.38	-1.05	0.55
32. Stone-Glass	2.06	0.20	1.77	0.30
33. Primary Metals	2.30	0.28	2.12	0.38
34. Fabricated Metals	2.46	0.19	2.26	0.29
35. Machinery	2.94	0.18	4.37	0.29
36. Electric Machinery	2.88	0.21	3.00	0.35
37. Transp. Equipment	1.49	0.31	1.17	0.46
38. Instruments	1.76	0.31	2.40	0.43
39. Miscellaneous	2.30	0.33	1.56	0.45

Note: Annual data for four-digit SIC manufacturing industries. The coefficients of the VAR(1) are estimated with a dummy variable for each industry. The standard errors and the impulse-responses are estimated following Luetkepohl (1991).

Table 5.2: *Variance decomposition of the SR model. Percentage of the forecast error explained by the sectoral shock.*

	First period		Long run	
	Y	*SR*	*Y*	*SR*
21. Tobacco	0.00	0.98	0.04	0.98
22. Textile Mill	0.00	0.98	0.02	0.97
23. Apparel	0.00	0.98	0.01	0.97
24. Lumber-Wood	0.00	1.00	0.03	0.95
25. Furniture	0.00	0.87	0.02	0.87
26. Paper	0.00	0.92	0.02	0.91
27. Printing	0.00	0.91	0.01	0.90
28. Chemicals	0.00	0.88	0.00	0.88
29. Petroleum-Coal	0.00	0.99	0.01	0.99
30. Rubber-Plastic	0.00	0.81	0.01	0.82
31. Leather	0.00	1.00	0.01	0.99
32. Stone-Glass	0.00	0.86	0.01	0.85
33. Primary Metals	0.00	0.91	0.01	0.91
34. Fabr. Metals	0.00	0.83	0.00	0.83
35. Machinery	0.00	0.79	0.05	0.76
36. Electric Machinery	0.00	0.83	0.00	0.83
37. Transportation Eqm.	0.00	0.95	0.00	0.95
38. Instruments	0.00	0.91	0.01	0.90
39. Miscellaneous	0.00	0.91	0.00	0.90

Note: Columns tagged *'Y'* contain the percentage of the forecast error variance decomposition of aggregate output explained by the sectoral shock. Columns under *'SR'* refer to the part of the SR explained by the sectoral shock. The contemporaneous sectoral component of aggregate output is imposed by the identifying assumption.

Table 5.3: *Granger Causality tests. SR model.*

	H_0: Y not GC SR	H_0: SR not GC Y
21. Tobacco	0.11	3.21
22. Textile Mill	11.01	17.49
23. Apparel	5.70	8.53
24. Lumber-Wood	19.02	14.14
25. Furniture	1.41	5.55
26. Paper	2.52	6.87
27. Printing	0.68	2.01
28. Chemicals	0.00	1.05
29. Petroleum-Coal	0.00	0.64
30. Rubber-Plastic	0.57	1.25
31. Leather	2.78	2.22
32. Stone-Glass	0.65	4.07
33. Primary Metals	0.13	5.32
34. Fabr. Metals	0.22	3.45
35. Machinery	31.44	47.17
36. Electric Machinery	0.09	0.01
37. Transportation Eqm.	0.44	1.13
38. Instruments	4.96	3.57
39. Miscellaneous	1.47	0.92

Note: The first column reports the F-test for the joint hypothesis that the coefficients of the variable SR and its lags in the equation for Y are zero. The second gives the test for variable Y in the equation for SR.

Table 5.4: *VAR of aggregate output growth and DSR. Response of productivity level to aggregate output (percent).*

	First period		Long run	
	Response	s.e.	Response	s.e.
21. Tobacco	0.91	0.57	1.20	0.97
22. Textile Mill	0.11	0.22	-1.02	0.41
23. Apparel	0.74	0.19	-0.10	0.32
24. Lumber-Wood	-0.64	0.29	-1.96	0.39
25. Furniture	2.33	0.32	1.88	0.50
26. Paper	1.22	0.22	0.07	0.35
27. Printing	1.28	0.29	1.10	0.40
28. Chemicals	1.99	0.25	1.91	0.43
29. Petroleum-Coal	1.00	0.62	0.22	1.07
30. Rubber-Plastic	1.96	0.33	2.29	0.51
31. Leather	-0.09	0.37	-1.00	0.55
32. Stone-Glass	1.70	0.16	1.79	0.28
33. Primary Metals	1.42	0.28	0.71	0.40
34. Fabr. Metals	2.20	0.16	2.27	0.27
35. Machinery	2.56	0.13	3.82	0.23
36. Electric Machinery	2.27	0.16	3.02	0.30
37. Transp. Equipment	1.19	0.20	1.11	0.36
38. Instruments	1.19	0.24	1.86	0.36
39. Miscellaneous	1.97	0.31	1.70	0.45

Note: Annual data for four-digit SIC manufacturing industries. The coefficients of the VAR(1) are estimated with a dummy variable for each industry. The standard errors and the impulse-responses are estimated following Luetkepohl (1991).

Table 5.5: *Variance decomposition of the DSR model. Percentage of the forecast error explained by the sectoral shock.*

	First period		Long run	
	Y	*DSR*	*Y*	*DSR*
21. Tobacco	0.00	0.98	0.05	0.97
22. Textile Mill	0.00	1.00	0.02	0.98
23. Apparel	0.00	0.98	0.02	0.97
24. Lumber-Wood	0.00	0.99	0.04	0.95
25. Furniture	0.00	0.86	0.02	0.86
26. Paper	0.00	0.93	0.04	0.90
27. Printing	0.00	0.96	0.00	0.95
28. Chemicals	0.00	0.91	0.00	0.92
29. Petroleum-Coal	0.00	0.98	0.01	0.97
30. Rubber-Plastic	0.00	0.79	0.01	0.79
31. Leather	0.00	1.00	0.02	0.98
32. Stone-Glass	0.00	0.85	0.00	0.86
33. Primary Metals	0.00	0.96	0.03	0.95
34. Fabr. Metals	0.00	0.82	0.01	0.82
35. Machinery	0.00	0.70	0.05	0.67
36. Electric Machinery	0.00	0.83	0.01	0.82
37. Transportation Equipment	0.00	0.93	0.00	0.93
38. Instruments	0.00	0.93	0.02	0.92
39. Miscellaneous	0.00	0.92	0.00	0.92

Note: Columns with *'Y'* contain the percentage of the forecast error variance decomposition of aggregate output explained by the sectoral shock. Columns under *'DSR'* refer to the part of the DSR explained by the sectoral shock. The contemporaneous sectoral component of aggregate output is imposed by the identifying assumption.

Table 5.6: *Granger Causality tests. DSR model.*

	H_0: Y not GC DSR	H_0: DSR not GC Y
21. Tobacco	0.05	4.30
22. Textile Mill	10.39	17.57
23. Apparel	10.60	16.04
24. Lumber-Wood	16.05	14.97
25. Furniture	1.18	6.73
26. Paper	16.07	16.19
27. Printing	0.01	1.74
28. Chemicals	0.63	0.15
29. Petroleum-Coal	0.91	0.95
30. Rubber-Plastic	0.69	1.33
31. Leather	3.47	5.80
32. Stone-Glass	0.11	2.07
33. Primary Metals	3.37	16.36
34. Fabr. Metals	0.19	6.67
35. Machinery	20.27	47.62
36. Electric Machinery	2.81	5.95
37. Transp. Equipment	0.55	0.29
38. Instruments	5.15	6.69
39. Miscellaneous	0.14	0.38

Note: The first column reports the F-test for the joint hypothesis that the coefficients of the variable DSR and its lags in the equation for Y are zero. The second gives the test for variable Y on equation for DSR.

Table 5.7: *VAR of aggregate output growth and sectoral output growth. Response of sectoral output level to aggregate output (percent).*

	First period		Long run	
	Response	s.e.	Response	s.e.
21. Tobacco	-0.28	0.75	-0.43	1.03
22. Textile Mill	4.09	0.52	2.13	0.78
23. Apparel	2.41	0.48	2.33	0.67
24. Lumber-Wood	4.31	0.60	3.49	0.98
25. Furniture	7.43	0.96	7.79	1.46
26. Paper	3.38	0.50	3.44	0.72
27. Printing	3.28	0.50	4.26	0.75
28. Chemicals	4.25	0.41	5.36	0.60
29. Petroleum-Coal	3.32	1.05	3.89	1.67
30. Rubber-Plastic	5.37	0.92	7.80	1.30
31. Leather	0.50	0.59	-0.13	0.88
32. Stone-Glass	5.19	0.39	5.91	0.64
33. Primary Metals	7.35	0.57	9.56	0.84
34. Fabr. Metals	6.11	0.46	8.62	0.89
35. Machinery	5.57	0.36	9.91	0.54
36. Electric Mach.	7.33	0.44	10.30	0.74
37. Transportation Eqm.	5.41	0.91	5.44	1.57
38. Instruments	3.84	0.59	7.09	1.04
39. Miscellaneous	4.38	0.51	3.98	0.80

Note: Annual data for four-digit SIC manufacturing industries. The coefficients of the VAR(1) are estimated with a dummy variable for each industry. The standard errors and the impulse-responses are estimated following Luetkepohl (1991).

Table 5.8: *Variance decomposition of the sectoral output model. Percentage of the forecast error explained by the sectoral shock.*

	First period		Long run	
	Y	y	Y	y
21. Tobacco	0.00	1.00	0.01	1.00
22. Textile Mill	0.00	0.92	0.01	0.91
23. Apparel	0.00	0.97	0.01	0.97
24. Lumber-Wood	0.00	0.89	0.03	0.89
25. Furniture	0.00	0.84	0.01	0.84
26. Paper	0.00	0.90	0.00	0.90
27. Printing	0.00	0.90	0.00	0.89
28. Chemicals	0.00	0.86	0.03	0.86
29. Petroleum-Coal	0.00	0.93	0.00	0.92
30. Rubber-Plastic	0.00	0.80	0.03	0.78
31. Leather	0.00	1.00	0.00	0.99
32. Stone-Glass	0.00	0.78	0.01	0.78
33. Primary Metals	0.00	0.78	0.02	0.77
34. Fabr. Metals	0.00	0.83	0.00	0.81
35. Machinery	0.00	0.81	0.12	0.73
36. Electric Machinery	0.00	0.76	0.01	0.73
37. Transportation Equipment	0.00	0.92	0.00	0.92
38. Instruments	0.00	0.88	0.02	0.83
39. Miscellaneous	0.00	0.87	0.00	0.87

Note: Columns with 'Y' contain the percentage of the forecast error variance decomposition of aggregate output explained by the sectoral shock. Columns under 'y' refer to the part of sectoral output explained by the sectoral shock. The contemporaneous sectoral component of aggregate output is imposed by the identifying assumption.

Table 5.9: *Granger Causality tests. Sectoral output model.*

	H_0: Y not GC y	H_0: y not GC Y
21. Tobacco	0.04	0.62
22. Textile Mill	7.59	8.95
23. Apparel	0.03	6.64
24. Lumber-Wood	1.93	10.44
25. Furniture	0.29	1.82
26. Paper	0.32	0.95
27. Printing	2.99	0.03
28. Chemicals	6.59	19.17
29. Petroleum-Coal	0.12	0.14
30. Rubber-Plastic	9.08	4.30
31. Leather	0.61	0.34
32. Stone-Glass	1.47	7.87
33. Primary Metals	16.34	13.71
34. Fabr. Metals	2.05	3.86
35. Machinery	101.02	137.73
36. Electric Machinery	18.24	10.92
37. Transportation Eqm.	0.18	0.93
38. Instruments	10.41	7.80
39. Miscellaneous	0.32	0.63

Note: The first column reports the F-test for the joint hypothesis that the coefficients of the variable y and its lags in the equation for Y are zero. The second gives the test for variable Y on equation for y.

Table 5.10: *VAR of aggregate output growth and labor growth. Response of the level of labor to aggregate output (percent).*

	First period		Long run	
	Response	s.e.	Response	s.e.
21. Tobacco	-0.93	0.75	-0.87	1.06
22. Textile Mill	3.29	0.42	3.06	0.64
23. Apparel	1.68	0.38	3.03	0.57
24. Lumber-Wood	5.28	0.55	6.62	0.99
25. Furniture	5.25	0.73	6.96	1.10
26. Paper	1.64	0.36	2.95	0.51
27. Printing	1.41	0.46	3.11	0.70
28. Chemicals	0.32	0.32	2.10	0.50
29. Petroleum-Coal	0.33	0.97	1.70	1.40
30. Rubber-Plastic	3.02	0.76	5.77	1.17
31. Leather	1.22	0.52	2.08	0.80
32. Stone-Glass	2.96	0.34	4.45	0.46
33. Primary Metals	3.33	0.37	6.00	0.51
34. Fabr. Metals	3.42	0.35	6.73	0.65
35. Machinery	1.85	0.27	5.46	0.38
36. Electric Mach.	3.95	0.33	7.53	0.51
37. Transportation Eqm.	3.97	0.68	5.72	1.23
38. Instruments	1.49	0.48	4.82	0.85
39. Miscellaneous	1.81	0.44	2.41	0.66

Note: Annual data for four-digit SIC manufacturing industries. The coefficients of the VAR(1) are estimated with a dummy variable for each industry. The standard errors and the impulse-responses are estimated following Luetkepohl (1991).

Table 5.11: *Variance decomposition of the sectoral labor model. Percentage of the forecast error explained by the sectoral shock.*

	First period		Long run	
	Y	n	Y	n
21. Tobacco	0.00	0.99	0.01	0.99
22. Textile Mill	0.00	0.92	0.00	0.92
23. Apparel	0.00	0.98	0.00	0.97
24. Lumber-Wood	0.00	0.81	0.00	0.80
25. Furniture	0.00	0.86	0.00	0.85
26. Paper	0.00	0.95	0.04	0.93
27. Printing	0.00	0.98	0.01	0.95
28. Chemicals	0.00	1.00	0.03	0.97
29. Petroleum-Coal	0.00	1.00	0.01	0.99
30. Rubber-Plastic	0.00	0.90	0.03	0.85
31. Leather	0.00	0.98	0.06	0.97
32. Stone-Glass	0.00	0.90	0.08	0.88
33. Primary Metals	0.00	0.89	0.14	0.83
34. Fabr. Metals	0.00	0.90	0.03	0.86
35. Machinery	0.00	0.96	0.14	0.83
36. Electric Machinery	0.00	0.87	0.05	0.79
37. Transportation Equipment	0.00	0.93	0.00	0.92
38. Instruments	0.00	0.97	0.04	0.89
39. Miscellaneous	0.00	0.97	0.00	0.97

Note: Columns with *'Y'* contain the percentage of the forecast error variance decomposition of aggregate output explained by the sectoral shock. Columns under *'n'* refer to the part of sectoral labor explained by the sectoral shock. The contemporaneous sectoral component of aggregate output is imposed by the identifying assumption.

Table 5.12: *Granger Causality tests. Sectoral labor model.*

	H_0: Y not GC n	H_0: n not GC Y
21. Tobacco	0.00	1.09
22. Textile Mill	0.14	0.11
23. Apparel	8.18	1.68
24. Lumber-Wood	0.49	0.37
25. Furniture	5.05	0.10
26. Paper	10.38	16.24
27. Printing	8.21	3.45
28. Chemicals	16.34	22.44
29. Petroleum-Coal	1.28	0.72
30. Rubber-Plastic	8.15	4.78
31. Leather	1.24	15.03
32. Stone-Glass	17.39	47.77
33. Primary Metals	41.12	99.10
34. Fabr. Metals	22.69	25.98
35. Machinery	133.09	169.51
36. Electric Mach.	77.90	51.74
37. Transportation Eqm.	1.07	0.95
38. Instruments	19.05	13.85
39. Miscellaneous	1.31	0.04

Note: The first column reports the F-test for the joint hypothesis that the coefficients of the variable n and its lags in the equation for Y are zero. The second gives the test for variable Y on equation for n.

Table 5.13: *VAR of aggregate output growth and materials growth. Response of the level of materials to aggregate output (percent).*

	First period		Long run	
	Response	s.e.	Response	s.e.
21. Tobacco	-0.66	0.87	-1.12	1.32
22. Textile Mill	3.99	0.57	2.20	0.86
23. Apparel	2.17	0.57	2.33	0.78
24. Lumber-Wood	5.24	0.58	6.63	1.04
25. Furniture	6.73	0.97	7.57	1.46
26. Paper	2.73	0.57	2.95	0.80
27. Printing	3.52	0.62	4.54	0.91
28. Chemicals	2.62	0.39	3.67	0.55
29. Petroleum-Coal	3.71	1.16	3.96	1.87
30. Rubber-Plastic	5.48	1.10	8.62	1.70
31. Leather	1.03	0.63	0.54	0.90
32. Stone-Glass	5.09	0.42	6.05	0.67
33. Primary Metals	7.36	0.62	9.94	0.93
34. Fabr. Metals	5.58	0.50	9.18	0.99
35. Machinery	4.68	0.39	9.29	0.59
36. Electric Mach.	7.02	0.64	10.20	1.01
37. Transportation Eqm.	4.78	0.99	4.83	1.69
38. Instruments	3.85	0.64	7.46	1.15
39. Miscellaneous	3.53	0.51	3.95	0.79

Note: Annual data for four-digit SIC manufacturing industries. The coefficients of the VAR(1) are estimated with a dummy variable for each industry. The standard errors and the impulse-responses are estimated following Luetkepohl (1991).

Table 5.14: *Variance decomposition of the sectoral materials model. Percentage of forecast error explained by the sectoral shock.*

	$t = 0$		$t = 10$	
	Y	m	Y	m
21. Tobacco	0.00	0.99	0.00	0.99
22. Textile Mill	0.00	0.94	0.01	0.93
23. Apparel	0.00	0.98	0.01	0.98
24. Lumber-Wood	0.00	0.83	0.01	0.83
25. Furniture	0.00	0.87	0.01	0.87
26. Paper	0.00	0.95	0.00	0.95
27. Printing	0.00	0.93	0.00	0.92
28. Chemicals	0.00	0.94	0.04	0.93
29. Petroleum-Coal	0.00	0.92	0.00	0.92
30. Rubber-Plastic	0.00	0.85	0.01	0.82
31. Leather	0.00	0.99	0.00	0.99
32. Stone-Glass	0.00	0.81	0.02	0.80
33. Primary Metals	0.00	0.81	0.04	0.80
34. Fabr. Metals	0.00	0.88	0.00	0.85
35. Machinery	0.00	0.88	0.08	0.80
36. Electric Machinery	0.00	0.89	0.00	0.87
37. Transportation Equipment	0.00	0.95	0.00	0.95
38. Instruments	0.00	0.90	0.01	0.85
39. Miscellaneous	0.00	0.91	0.00	0.91

Note: Columns with 'Y' contain the percentage of the forecast error variance decomposition of aggregate output explained by the sectoral shock. Columns under 'm' refer to the part of materials explained by the sectoral shock. The contemporaneous sectoral component of aggregate output is imposed by the identifying assumption.

Table 5.15: *Granger Causality tests. Sectoral materials model.*

	H_0: Y not GC m	H_0: m not GC Y
21. Tobacco	0.16	0.45
22. Textile Mill	5.04	4.40
23. Apparel	0.35	8.93
24. Lumber-Wood	0.64	4.26
25. Furniture	0.91	1.74
26. Paper	0.50	3.14
27. Printing	2.75	1.30
28. Chemicals	6.67	27.55
29. Petroleum-Coal	0.01	0.00
30. Rubber-Plastic	5.82	1.55
31. Leather	0.25	0.05
32. Stone-Glass	2.34	12.62
33. Primary Metals	13.31	22.22
34. Fabr. Metals	7.33	4.00
35. Machinery	94.74	87.81
36. Electric Machinery	13.74	3.42
37. Transportation Eqm.	0.08	1.05
38. Instruments	10.65	3.39
39. Miscellaneous	0.39	0.38

Note: The first column reports the F-test for the joint hypothesis that the coefficients of the variable m and its lags in the equation for Y are zero. The second gives the test for variable Y on equation for m.

Appendix 2: Responses of Cumulated SR and DSR to a Shock in Aggregate Activity.

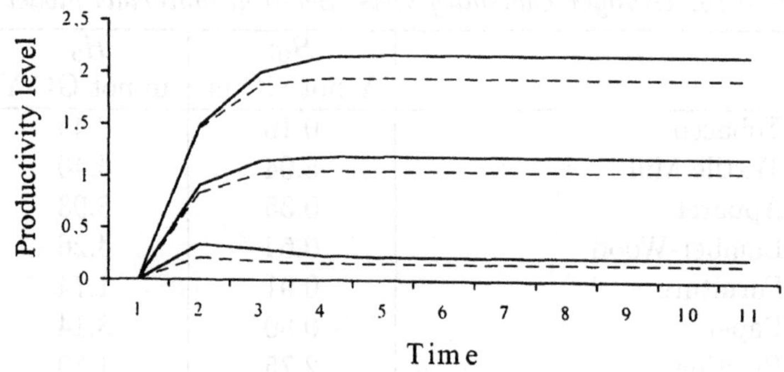

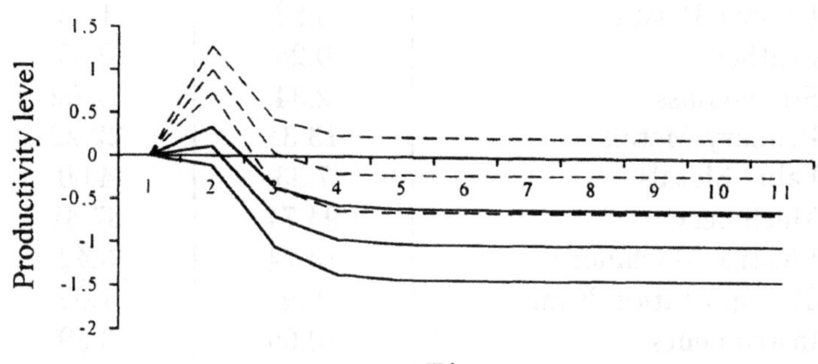

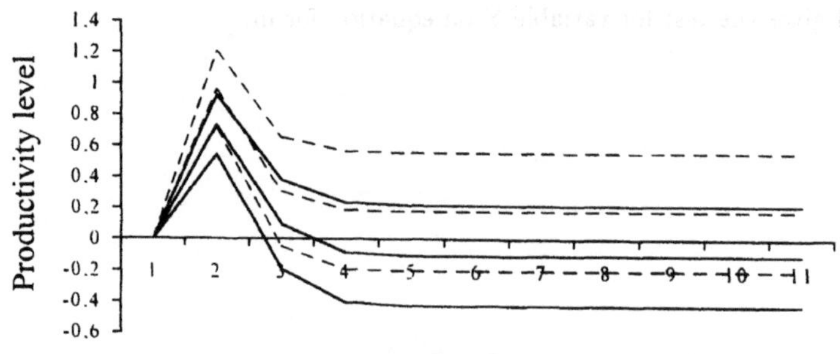

Sector 24. SR (---) and DSR

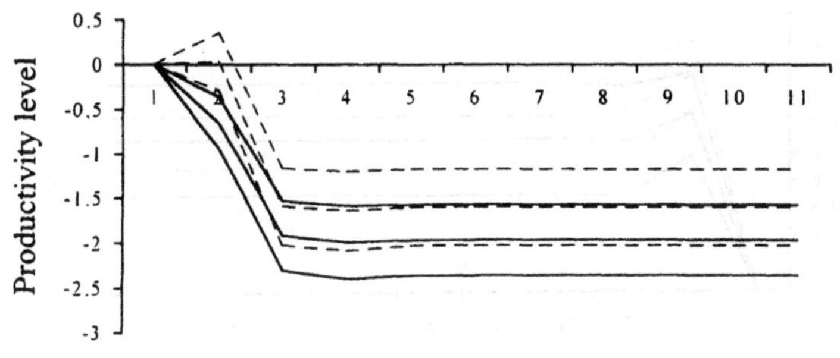

Sector 25. SR (---) and DSR

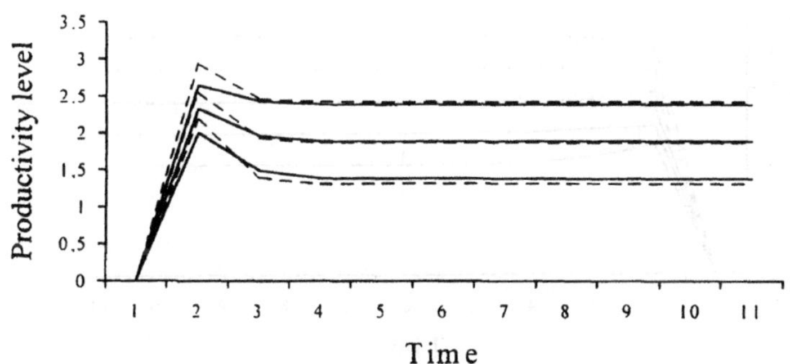

Sector 26. SR (---) and DSR

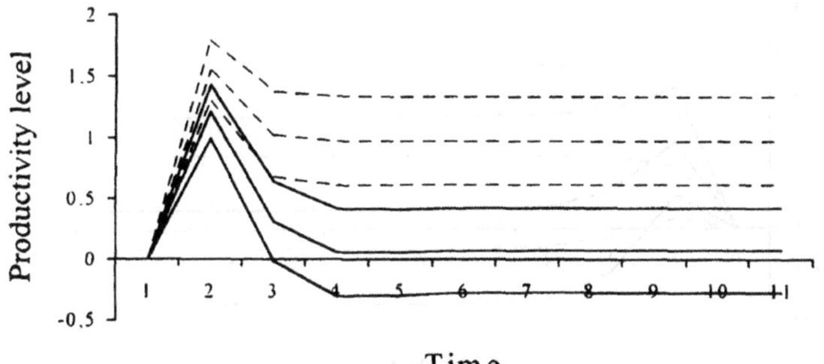

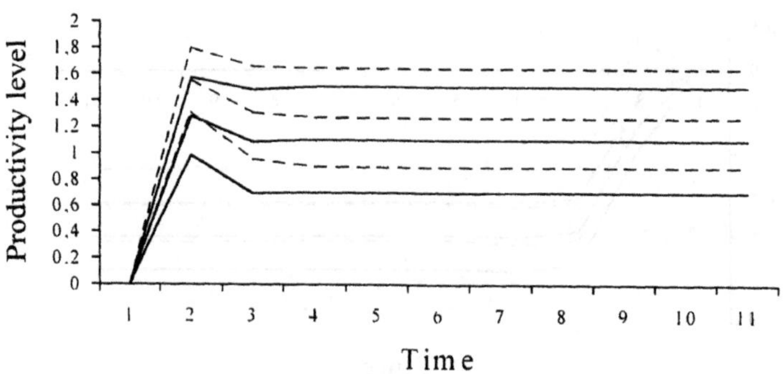
Sector 27. SR (---) and DSR
Productivity level
2
1.8
1.6
1.4
1.2
1
0.8
0.6
0.4
0.2
0
1
2
3
4
5
6
7
8
9
10
11
Time

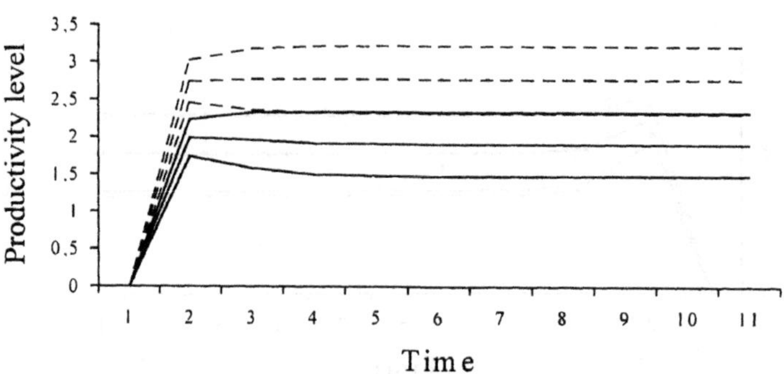
Sector 28. SR (---) and DSR
Productivity level
3.5
3
2.5
2
1.5
1
0.5
0
1
2
3
4
5
6
7
8
9
10
11
Time

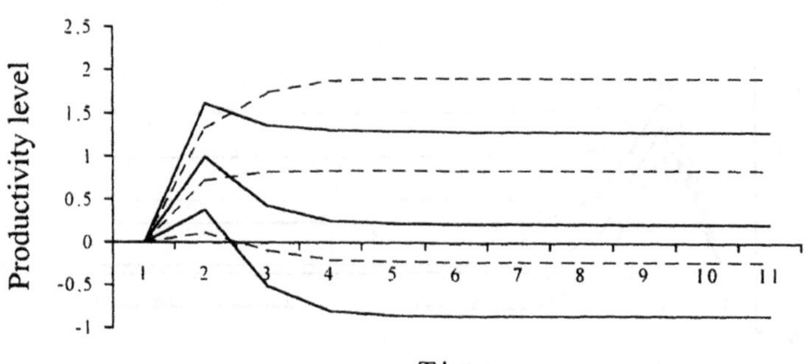
Sector 29. SR (---) and DSR
Productivity level
2.5
2
1.5
1
0.5
0
-0.5
-1
1
2
3
4
5
6
7
8
9
10
11
Time

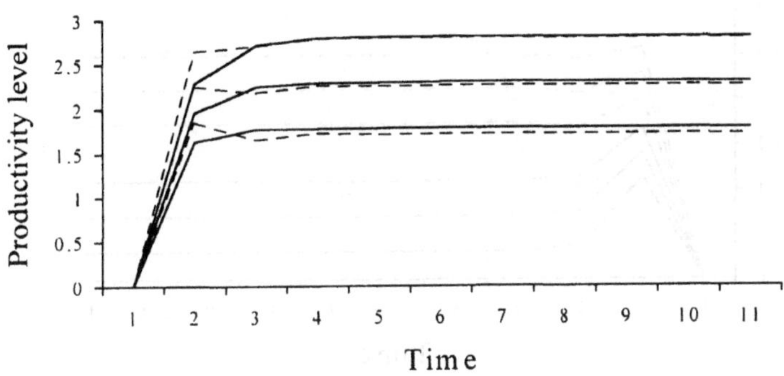
Sector 30. SR (---) and DSR
Productivity level
3
2.5
2
1.5
1
0.5
0
1 2 3 4 5 6 7 8 9 10 11
Time

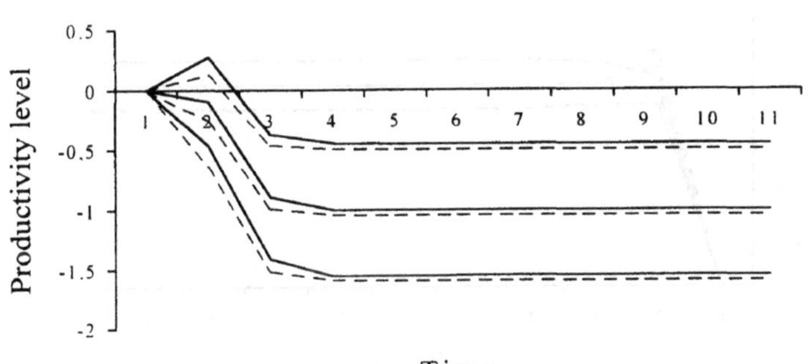
Sector 31. SR (---) and DSR
Productivity level
0.5
0
-0.5
-1
-1.5
-2
1 2 3 4 5 6 7 8 9 10 11
Time

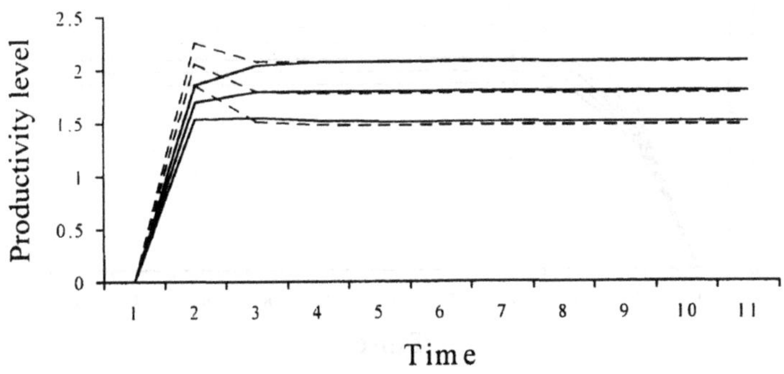
Sector 32. SR (---) and DSR
Productivity level
2.5
2
1.5
1
0.5
0
1 2 3 4 5 6 7 8 9 10 11
Time

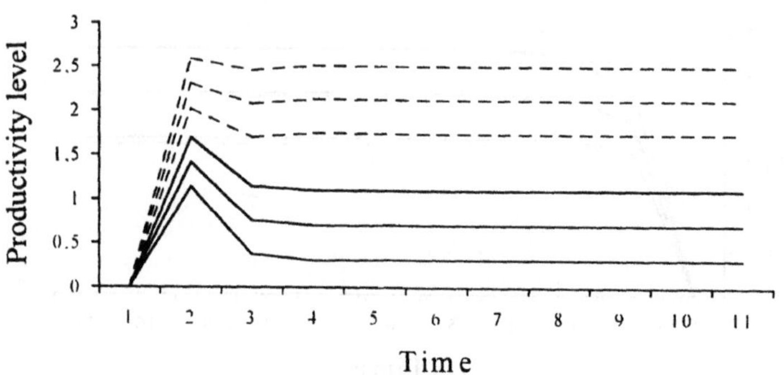
Sector 33. SR (---) and DSR
Productivity level
3
2,5
2
1,5
1
0,5
0
1 2 3 4 5 6 7 8 9 10 11
Time

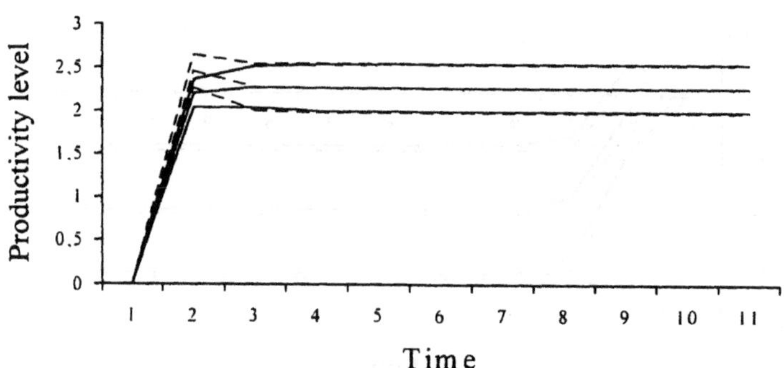
Sector 34. SR (---) and DSR
Productivity level
3
2,5
2
1,5
1
0,5
0
1 2 3 4 5 6 7 8 9 10 11
Time

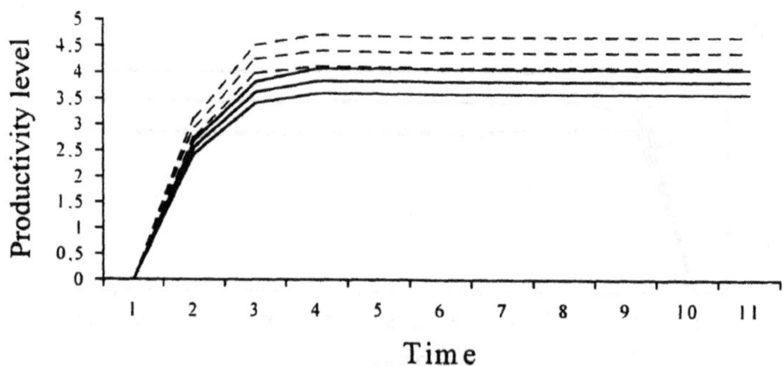
Sector 35. SR (---) and DSR
Productivity level
5
4,5
4
3,5
3
2,5
2
1,5
1
0,5
0
1 2 3 4 5 6 7 8 9 10 11
Time

Sector 36. SR (---) and DSR

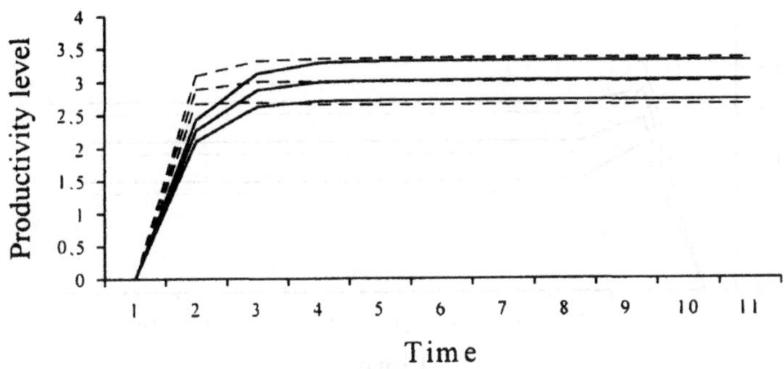

Sector 37. SR (---) and DSR

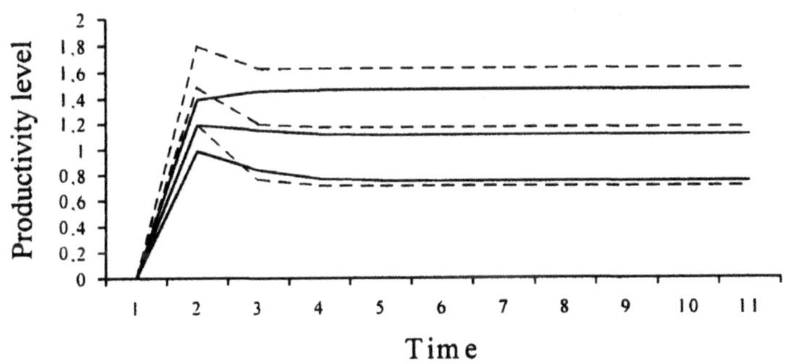

Sector 38. SR (---) and DSR

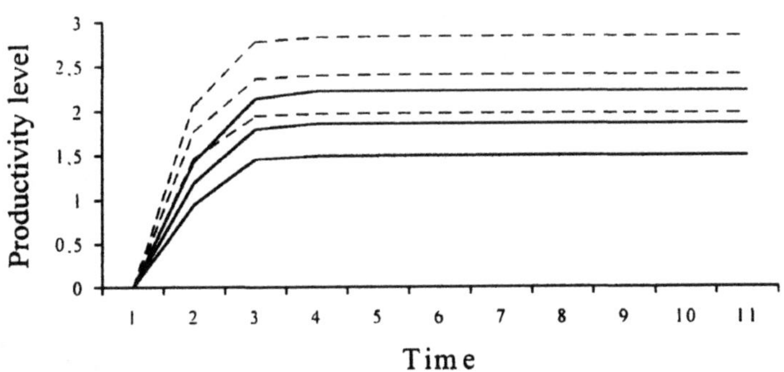

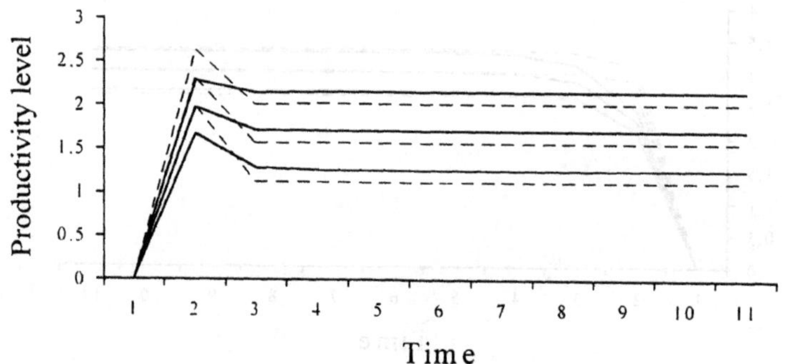
Sector 39. SR (---) and DSR
Productivity level
3
2.5
2
1.5
1
0.5
0
1
2
3
4
5
6
7
8
9
10
11
Time

Appendix 3: Responses of the Level of Sectoral Output, Labor and Materials to a Shock in Aggregate Activity.

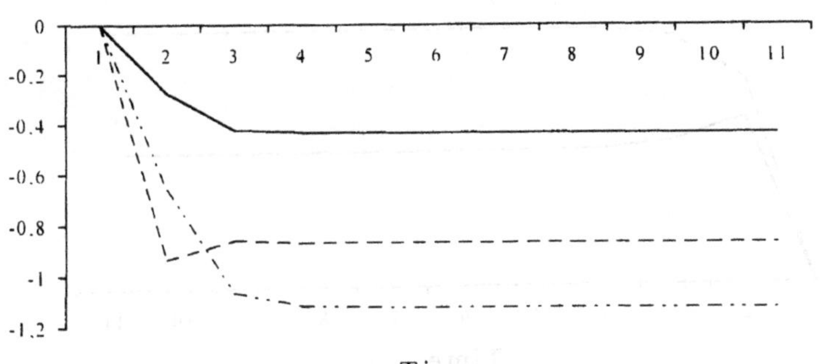

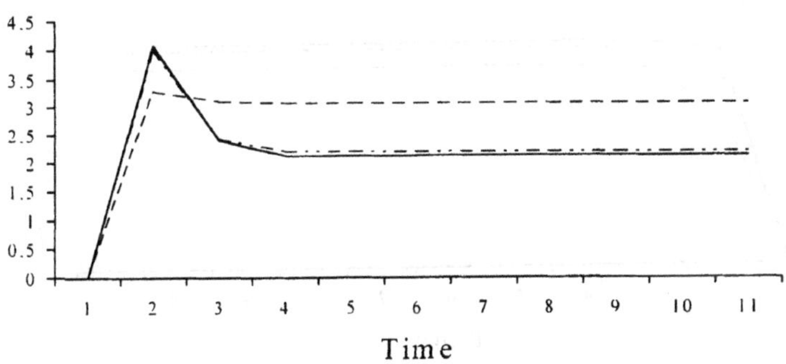

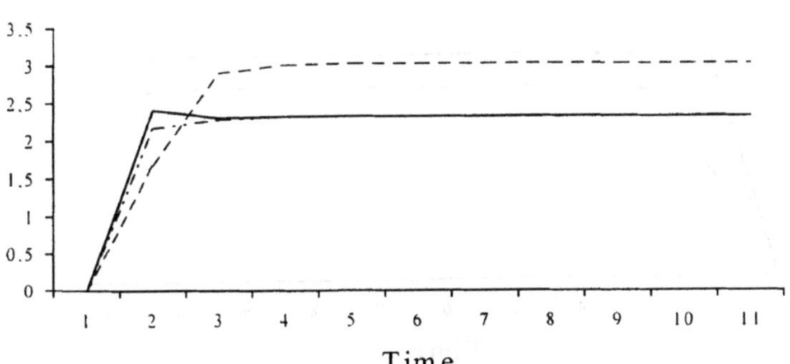

Sector 24. y, n (---) and m (-..-)

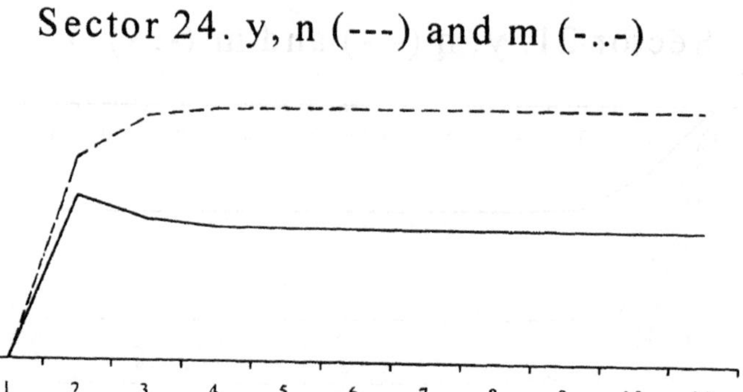

Sector 25. y, n (---) and m (-..-)

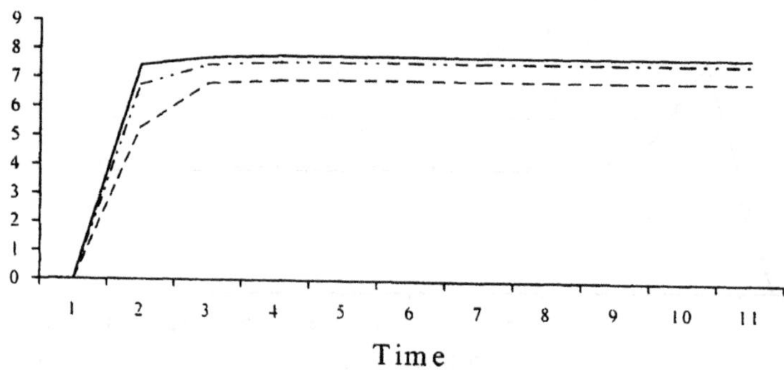

Sector 26. y, n (---) and m (-..-)

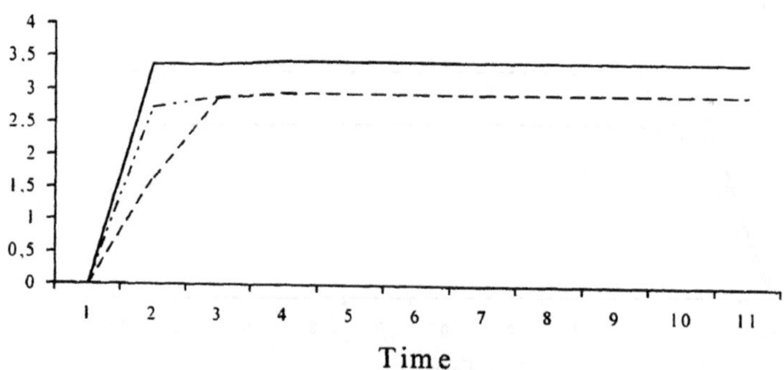

Sector 27. y, n (---) and m (-..-)

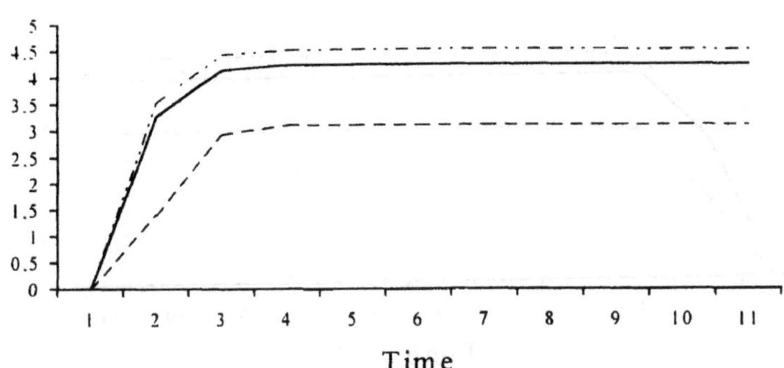

Sector 28. y, n (---) and m (-..-)

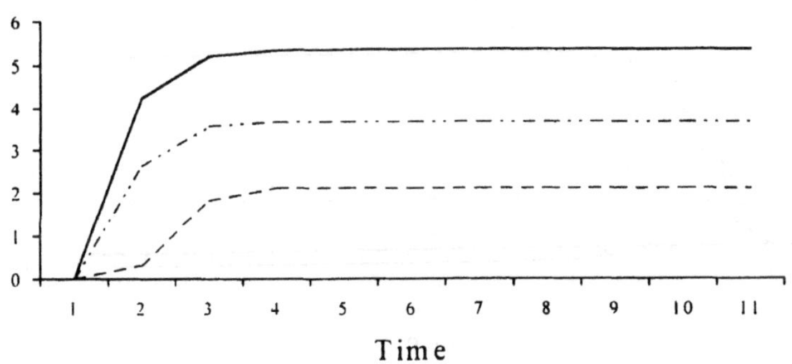

Sector 29. y, n (---) and m (-..-)

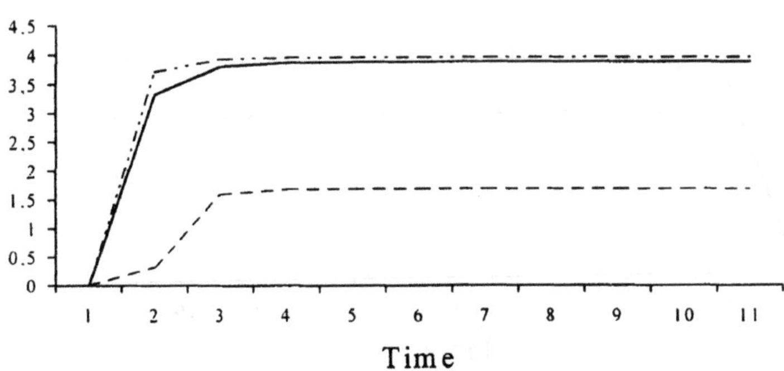

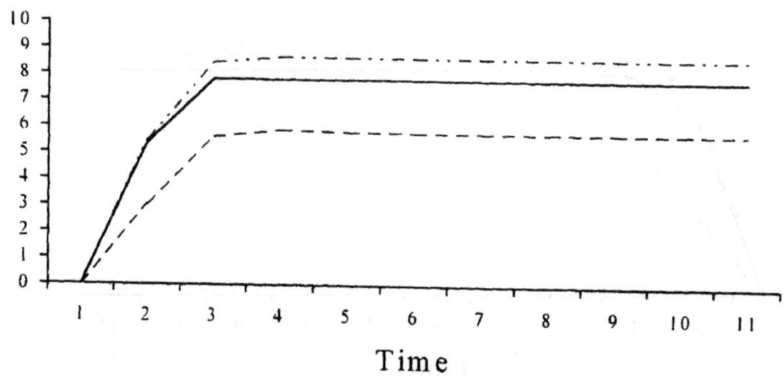
Sector 30. y, n (---) and m (-..-)
10
9
8
7
6
5
4
3
2
1
0
1 2 3 4 5 6 7 8 9 10 11
Time

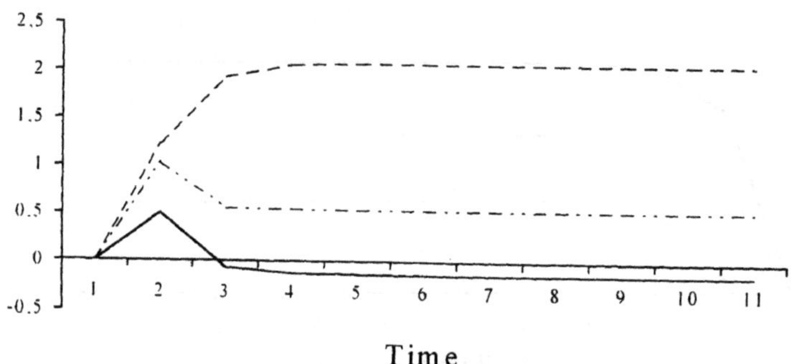
Sector 31. SR (---) and DSR
2.5
2
1.5
1
0.5
0
-0.5
1 2 3 4 5 6 7 8 9 10 11
Time

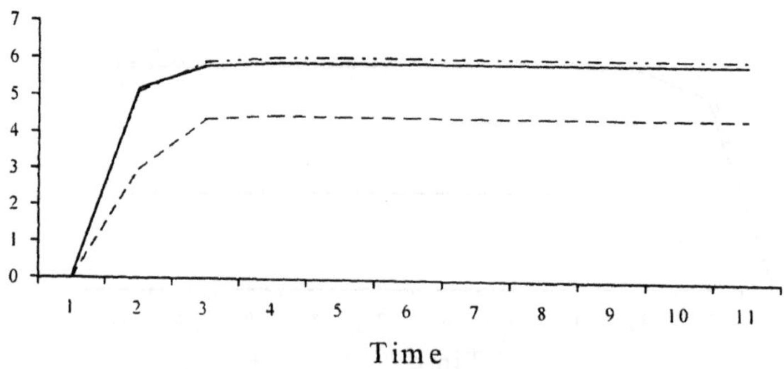
Sector 32. y, n (---) and m (-..-)
7
6
5
4
3
2
1
0
1 2 3 4 5 6 7 8 9 10 11
Time

Sector 33. y, n (---) and m (-..-)

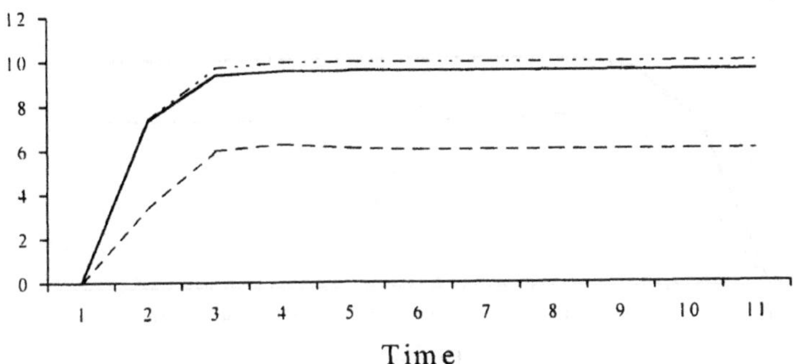

Sector 34. y, n (--) and m (-..-)

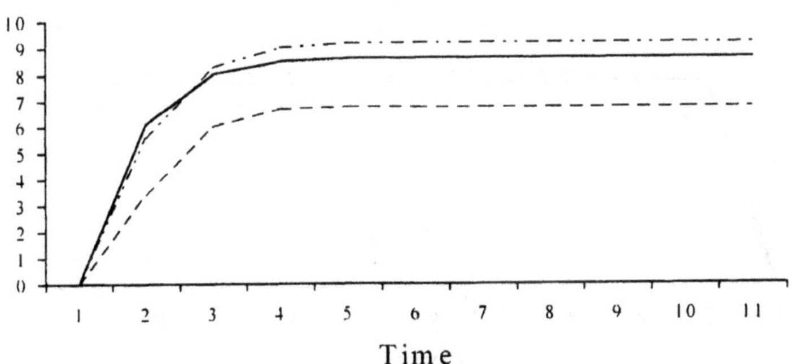

Sector 35. y, n (---) and m (-..-)

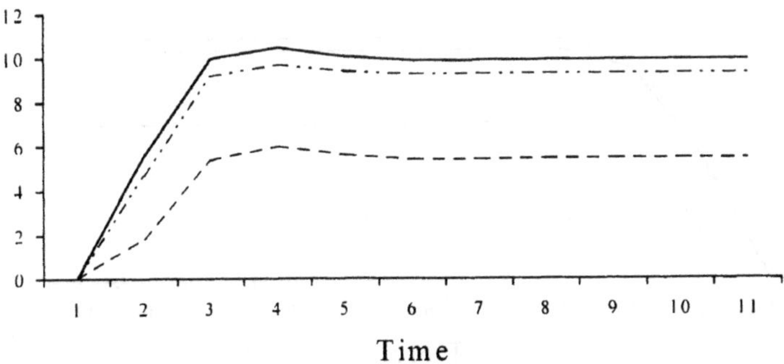

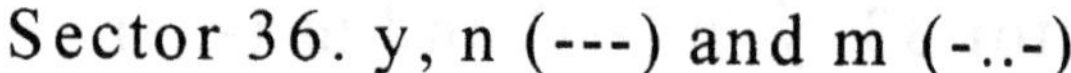

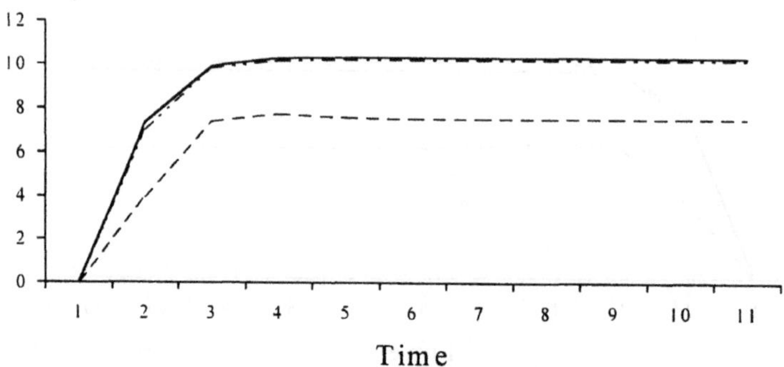

Sector 37. y, n (---) and m (-..-)

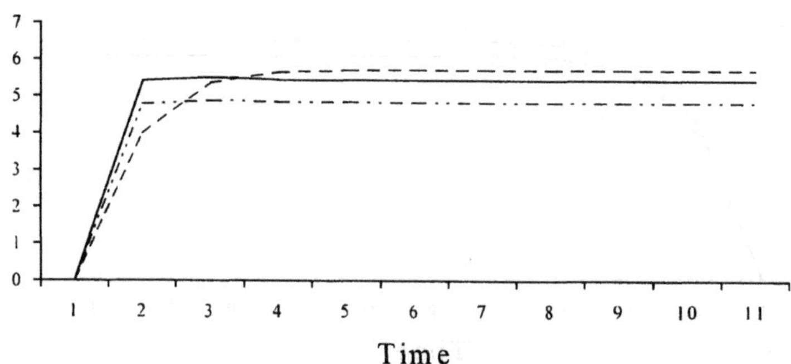

Sector 38. y, n (---) and m (-..-)

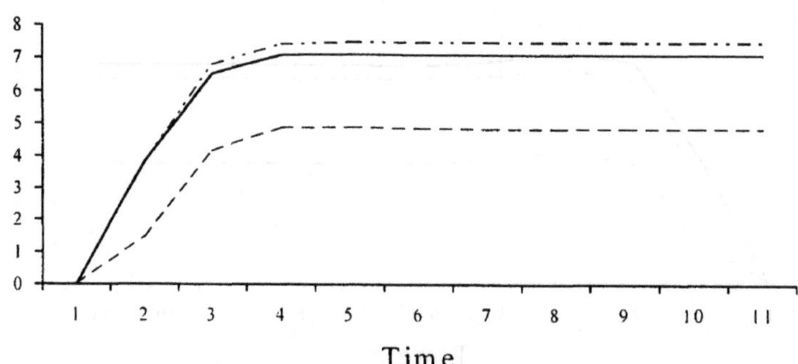

Sector 39. y, n (---) and m (-..-)

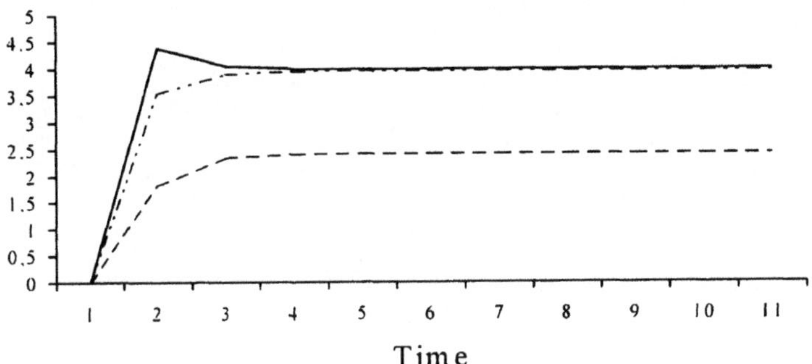
5
4.5
4
3.5
3
2.5
2
1.5
1
0.5
0
1
2
3
4
5
6
7
8
9
10
11
Time

Bibliography

Abbott, T., Z. Griliches and J. Hausman (1989). "Short Run Movements in Productivity: Market Power vs. Capacity Utilization." Manuscript.

Aghion, P. and G. Saint-Paul (1991). "On the Virtues of Bad Times." *CEPR Working Paper* No. 578. London: Center for Economic Policy Research.

Baily, M.N. (1990). "Comments: Competition, Increasing Returns, and the Solow Productivity Residual," in *Growth, Productivity, Unemployment*, P. Diamond, ed. Cambridge (MA): The MIT Press.

Bartelsman, E., R.J. Caballero and R.K. Lyons (1994). "Customer and Supplier-Driven Externalities." *American Economic Review* 84: 1075-84.

Basu, S. (1995). "Intermediate Goods and Business Cycles: Implications for Productivity and Welfare." *American Economic Review* 85 (3): 512-531.

Basu, S. (1996). "Procyclical Productivity: Increasing Returns or Cyclical Utilization?." *Quarterly Journal of Economics* 111: 719-751.

Basu, S. and J.G. Fernald (1994). "Constant returns and small markups in US manufacturing." *International Finance Discussion Paper* No. 483. Washington, DC: Board of Governors of the Federal Reserve System.

Basu, S. and J.G. Fernald (1995). "Are apparent productive spillovers a figment of specification error?" *Journal of Monetary Economics* 36: 165-188.

Bean, C. (1990). "Endogenous Growth and the Procyclical Behaviour of Productivity." *European Economic Review* 34: 355-363.

Bernanke, B.S. and M.L. Parkinson (1991). "Procyclical Labor Productivity and Competing Theories of the Business Cycle: Some Evidence from Interwar U.S. Manufacturing Industries." *Journal of Political Economy* 99: 439-459.

Burnside, C. (1996). "Production Function Regressions, Returns to Scale, and Externalities." *Journal of Monetary Economics* 37: 177-201.

Burnside, C., M. Eichenbaum and S. Rebelo (1993), "Labour Hoarding and the Business Cycle." *Journal of Political Economy* 101: 245-73.

Burnside, C., M. Eichenbaum and S. Rebelo (1996), "Capital Utilization and Returns to Scale," in *NBER Macroeconomics Annual*, J. Rotemberg and B. Bernanke, eds. Cambridge (MA): MIT Press.

Caballero, R.J. and M.L. Hammour (1994). "The Cleansing Effect of Recessions." *American Economic Review* 84 (5): 1350-1368.

Caballero, R.J. and R.K. Lyons (1990). "Internal versus External Economies in European Industry." *European Economic Review* 34: 805-830.

Caballero, R.J. and R.K. Lyons (1992). "External Effects in U.S. Procyclical Productivity." *Journal of Monetary Economics* 29: 209-25.

Diamond, P. (1982). "Aggregate Demand Management in Search Equilibrium." *Journal of Political Economy* 90: 881-894.

Domowitz, I., R.G. Hubbard and B.C. Petersen (1988). "Market Structure and Cyclical Fluctuations in US Manufacturing." *Review of Economics and Statistics* 70: 55-66.

Fay, J.A. and J.L. Medoff (1985). "Labor and Output over the Business Cycle: Some Direct Evidence." *American Economic Review* 75: 638-55.

Galí, J. and M.L. Hammour (1993). "Long Run Effects of Business Cycles." Columbia University. Manuscript.

Gordon, R. (1990). "Are Procyclical Productivity Fluctuations a Figment of Measurement Errors?" Northwestern University. Manuscript.

Gray, W.B. (1989). "Productivity Database." Clark University. Manuscript.

Hall, R.E. (1988). "The Relation between Price and Marginal Cost in U.S. Industry." *Journal of Political Economy* 96: 921-947.

Hall, R.E. (1990). "Invariance Properties of Solow's Productivity Residual." in *Growth, Productivity, Unemployment*, P. Diamond, ed. Cambridge (MA): The MIT Press.

Hall, R.E. (1991). "Labor Demand, Labor Supply and Employment Volatility," in *NBER Macroeconomics Annual 1991*, O.J. Blanchard and S. Fischer, eds. Cambridge (MA): The MIT Press.

Holm, S. (1979). "A Simple Sequentially Rejective Multiple Test Procedure." *Scandinavian Journal of Statistics* 6: 65-70.

Holtz-Eakin, D., W. Newey and H.S. Rosen (1988). "Estimating Vector Autoregressions with Panel Data." *Econometrica* 56: 1047-1070.

Hsiao, C. (1986). *Analysis of Panel Data.* Cambridge (UK): Cambridge University Press.

Jimeno, J.F. (1989). "Productivity Shocks, Demand Shocks and Economic Fluctuations: and Empirical Investigation with a Structural Approach." Massachussets Institute of Technology. Manuscript.

Jorgenson, D.W., F.M. Gollop and B.M. Fraumeni (1987). *Productivity and US Economic growth*, Cambridge (MA): The MIT Press.

Kiyotaki, N. (1988). "Multiple Expectional Equilibria Under Monopolistic Competition." *Quarterly Journal of Economics* 103: 695-714.

Long, J.B. and Ch.I. Plosser (1983). "Real Business Cycles". *Journal of Political Economy* 91: 39-69.

Luetkepohl, H. (1991). *Introduction to Multiple Time Series Analysis*, Berlin: Springer-Verlag.

Marchetti, D. (1994). "Procyclical Productivity, Externalities and Labor Hoarding: A Reexamination of Evidence from U.S. Manufacturing." *EUI Working Paper in Economics* No. 94-13. Florence: European University Institute.

Martin, S. (1993). *Advanced Industrial Economics*, Cambridge (MA): Blackwells.

Morrison, C.J. (1988). "Quasi-fixed Inputs in U.S. and Japanese Manufacturing: A Generalized Leontief Restricted Cost Function Approach." *Review of Economics and Statistics* 70: 275-287.

Morrison, C.J. (1992). "Markups in US and Japanese Manufacturing: A Short-Run Econometric Analysis." *Journal of Business and Economic Statistics* 10 (1): 51-63.

Murphy, K.M., A. Schleifer and R.W. Vishny (1989). "Industrialization and the Big Push." *Journal of Political Economy* 97: 1003-26.

Norrbin, S.C. (1993). "The Relation between Price and Marginal Cost in U.S. Industry: A Contradiction." *Journal of Political Economy* 101 (6): 1149-64.

Oi, W. (1962). "Labour as a Quasi-Fixed Input." *Journal of Political Economy* 70: 538-555.

Pelloni, A. (1997). "Nominal Rigidities, Endogenous Growth and the Business Cycle." *Economic Journal* 107 (441): 467-474.

Perron (1989). "The Great Crash, the Oil Price Shock, and the Unit Root Hypothesis." *Econometrica* 57: 1361-1401.

Prescott, J. (1986). "Theory Ahead of Business Cycle Measurement." *Federal Reserve Bank of Minneapolis Quarterly Review*, Fall 1986: 9-22.

Ramey, V. (1991). "Non-Convex Costs and the Behavior of Inventories." *Journal of Political Economy* 99: 306-334.

Roeger, W. (1995). "Can Imperfect Competition Explain the Difference between Primal and Dual Productivity Measures? Estimates for U.S. Manufacturing." *Journal of Political Economy* 103 (2): 316-330.

Rotemberg, J. and L. Summers (1990). "Inflexible prices and procyclical productivity." *Quarterly Journal of Economics* 105: 851-874.

Rotemberg, J. and M. Woodford (1991). "Markups and the Business Cycle." in *NBER Macroeconomics Annual 1991*, O.J. Blanchard and S. Fischer, eds. Cambridge (MA): The MIT Press.

Rotemberg, J. and M. Woodford (1992). "Imperfect Competition and the Effects of Energy Price Increases on Economic Activity." *IGIER Working Paper* No. 27. Milan: Innocenzo Gasparini Institute for Economic Research.

Saint-Paul, G. (1993). "Productivity Growth and the Structure of the Business Cycle." *European Economic Review* 37: 861-890.

Sbordone, A. (1996). "Cyclical productivity in a model of labor hoarding." *Journal of Monetary Economics* 38: 331-361.

Sbordone, A. (1997). "Interpreting the Procyclical Productivity of Manufacturing Sectors: External Effects or Labor Hoarding?" *Journal of Money, Credit and Banking* 29 (1): 26-45.

Schumpeter, J.A. (1939). *Business Cycles.* New York: McGraw-Hill.

Shapiro, M.D. (1987). "Are Cyclical Fluctuations in Productivity Due More to Supply Shocks or Demand Shocks?" *American Economic Review Papers and Proceedings* 77: 118-124.

Shea, J. (1992). "Accident Rates, Labor Effort and the Business Cycle." University of Wisconsin. Manuscript.

Stadler, G.W. (1990). "Business Cycle Models with Endogenous Technology." *American Economic Review* 80 (4): 763-778.

Solow, R.M. (1957). "Technical Change and the Aggregagte Production Function." *Review of Economics and Statistics* 39: 312-20.

Summers, L.H. (1986). "Some Skeptical Observations on Real Business Cycle Theory." *Federal Reserve Bank of Minneapolis Quarterly Review* 10: 23-26.

Waldmann, R. (1991). "Implausible Results or Implausible data? Anomalies in the Construction of Value Added Data and Implications for the Estimation of Price-Cost Margins." *Journal of Political Economy* 99 (6): 1315-1328.

Programs

All the econometric calculations performed in this book have been done with MATLAB, a mathematics program that allows for all kind of operations with matrices as the basic unit. The main reason for using it is that it allows for much more flexibility than standard econometric packages, especially those designed for large panel datasets. In particular, there are two things that programs for panel data do not allow for: one is the calculation of the robust standard errors of the regression coefficients when we use instrumental variables in a fixed-effects estimation. The other is the estimation of VAR models with panel data. Standard programs for panel data are not designed for this, and although it is possible to estimate the VAR coefficients, any extension like the orthogonalization of the residuals or the derivation of the impulse responses is not usually possible with such packages. The panel-VAR model could also be done with programs more adapted for time series, but the handling of the sectoral dummies is somewhat cumbersone in this case.

Because of these reasons I decided to write my own library of "macros" in MATLAB. Most of them are what in MATLAB language are called "functions", and included in files with the extension *".m"*. They are nothing other than standard calculations that take some inputs and give back some outputs. These functions can be used as standard in-built commands of MATLAB and be used inside other MATLAB functions or programs. In my case many of the functions perform the same action repeatedly for the different groups within a panel of data, simplifying considerably all the operations.

The main two programs used for the calculations carried out in this research are *xvarsec.m* and *xpanel.m*. The former estimates a VAR model with panel data and also calculates some other things, like the canonical and orthogonal impulse response functions with confidence bands, the forecast error variance decomposition and the historical decompositions. It also plots the impulse responses of the integrated variables (the variables in levels for the case in which the VAR has been estimated in first differences). It estimates the VAR coefficients with one or two dummies (in order to introduce structural breaks in the constant) or with instrumental variables.

The program *xpanel.m* performs standard regressions with panel data, with different options. It allows for two-stage least squares or ordinary least squares estimator. There are three options for possible restrictions between the parameters: All the coefficients are equal, only the slope coefficients are equal (fixed effects), or all the coefficients are free. The two features that distinguish it from standard packages are the calculation of robust standard errors for any combination of these options (allowing for cross-covariances between groups to be different and *also* heteroskedastic) and the incorporation of the overidentification test for the instrumental variables estimation (used in Chapter 3). For the calculation of robust standard errors, it uses two separate *macros*: (*xwhite.m* and *xwhitear.m*.

I present below a description of *xpanel.m* and *xvarsec.m*, and of those other *macros* that are called by those two programs. The description can be used as a short manual for the library. The rest of the macros written for this library are also cited, with a brief description of what they do. They do not need to be understood for the utilization of *xpanel.m* and *xvarsec.m*, but they can be used by the reader for expanding the library, since they are especially suited for operations with panels of data. A diskette with the whole library can be sent to the reader upon request (provisional e-mail address: jdiaz@databasedm.es; mail address: OECD, Economics Division, 2 Rue André Pascal, 75775 Paris Cedex 16, France).

All these *'m functions'* have a name that start with a letter x, in order to distinguish them from in-built functions in MATLAB. The format of all functions is the following:

$$[K1, K2...Kn] = xname(A1, A2, ..., An)$$

where *K1,...,Kn* are the outputs of the function and *A1,...,An* are the inputs. The expression *xname* refers to the name of the function. In what follows, we will use the following notation for the explanation of the programs:

- T is the time spread of the panel.
- N is the number of cross-sectional groups –in our case, industries.
- k is the number of independent variables in an equation.
- K is the number of variables in a VAR model.
- w is the number of instrumental variables.
- *K1, K2... Kn* will be the names of the matrices with the output.

In most programs one of the inputs is a matrix that includes all the data in the panel. This matrix should always be organized in the following way: every column correspond to a different variable, and every row to an observation. In the first T rows of the panel we must include the time series observations corresponding to the first group or individual; in the second set of T rows the ones corresponding to the second group of individuals; and so on, until N groups.

MAIN PROGRAMS

xpanel.m *xpanel.m*

Purpose:

It performs Multiple Least Squares estimation or Two-Stages Least Squares (2SLS), with an option for carrying out the overidentification test for the instrumental variables. It uses other macros described below: *xoverid.m*, *x1step.m*, as well as macros for calculating robust standard errors, *xwhite.m* and *xwhitear.m*.

Format:

[K1,K2,K3,K4,K5]=xpanel(H,T,fe,wh,iv,W,ov,s1,AR)

Inputs:

H: (TxN)x(k+1) matrix with the data. The first column must have the independent variable Y, and the last k columns the regressors X.

T: Number of periods in the panel.

fe: Option toggle that can take three values: If fe=0 (default), all the coefficients are restricted to be same among groups. If fe=1, only the slopes are restricted (fixed effects case). If fe=2, no restrictions are imposed among groups.

wh: Option toggle that can take three values. If wh=0, the program does not return the standard errors and t-values (and therefore saves computational time). If wh=1 (default), it gives normal standard errors, i.e. assuming common variance for all time periods and groups. If wh=2, it returns robust standard errors, assuming different contemporaneous variances for each group and period. If wh=3, it returns standard errors that are robust to cross-correlation among groups, and to autocorrelation of order AR within groups, where AR is another input (see below).

iv: Option toggle with two possible values. If iv=0 (default), it uses multivariate least squares. If iv=1, it uses 2SLS.

W: (TxN)xW matrix with the instruments, if any. Each column must include a different instrument.

ov: Option toggle with two possible values. If *ov*=1, it creates output matrix K5 with all the data needed for the overidentification test of the instruments (see below output K5). If *ov*=0 it leaves K5 empty. K5 will be used in the program *xoverid.m*, where the test is performed.

s1: Option toggle with two options. If $s1$=0 (default), it uses fixed effects in the first stage of the 2SLS estimation. If $s1$=1, it runs individual regressions for each sector in the first stage 2SLS. This option is only meaningful when fe=1 and iv=1.

AR: Order of autoregression for which the standard errors are robust in case the option wh takes the value 3.

Outputs:

K1: Matrix of order kx3 that gives in the first column the estimated coefficients, in the second column their standard errors, and in the third column the t-values of the null hypothesis that the coefficient is equal to zero. If wh=0, it only gives the first column. Each of the k rows correspond to one regressor.

K2: 1x2 vector with the R^2 coefficient and the corrected R^2.

K3: (TxN)x1 vector with the estimated errors. The first T numbers correspond to the first group, the second T to the second group and so on.

K4: (TxN)x1 vector with the estimated errors plus the constant for each group (in case we have used fixed effects).

K5: (TxN)x(1+k+w) matrix which has in the first column the independent Y variable of the regression, in the next k columns the instrumented regressors that result from the first stage of the 2SLS procedure and in the last w columns the original instruments. The whole matrix is used as an input for the function *xoverid.m*, that performs the overidentification test.

Purpose:

It performs the overidentification test for the instruments used in 2SLS estimation, described in section 3.4.2. It takes matrix K5 from the program *xpanel* as an input and returns a matrix with the t-values of the test for each instrument.

Format:

[K1]=xoverid(A)

Inputs:

A: (TxN)x(1+k+w) matrix given as an output K5 in *xpanel.m*. It contains the independent variable in the first column, the instrumented regressors in the next k columns, and the instruments in the last w columns. Each row refers to one observation, ordered in N groups with T observations each.

Outputs:

K1: 1xw vector with the t-value of the test for each instrument.

x1step.m

x1step.m

Purpose:

It is called from *xpanel.m* and it runs the first step of 2SLS.

Format:

[K1,K2]=x1step(Y,X,T,d)

Inputs:

Y: (NxT)xk vector with the k regressors, ordered as usual.

X: (NxT)xw matrix with the w instruments.

T: Number of time periods.

d: Option toggle with three alternatives. If *d*=0, it restricts all the coefficients in the first stage to be equal across groups. If *d*=1 it applies fixed effects in the first stage. If *d*=2 it runs independent OLS in the first stage.

Outputs:

K1: (NxT)xk matrix with the instrumented regressors, needed for the second stage of 2SLS.

K2: Matrix of order (kxw) with the estimated coefficients of the first stage. Each row corresponds to a different regressor, and each column to a different instrument.

Purpose:

Estimates a VAR model with panel data using dummy variables and calculates impulse responses, variance decompositions and historical decompositions. It calls other macros described below: *xvarse.m*, *xvardec.m*, *xplotma.m*, *xmar.m* and *xmarlev.m*.

Format:

[K1,K2,...K15]=xvarsec(G,T,P,iv,pl,IVAR,W,d)

Inputs:

G: (TxN)xk matrix with the k variables of the VAR, one in each column.

T: Number of time periods. If we need two different dummy variables to introduce a structural break in the sample, then T is a 1x2 vector containing the number of time units of the first and the second sub-periods in the 2 respective columns.

P: Lag order of the VAR.

iv: Option toggle to choose the estimation method. If *iv*=0, fixed effects estimation. If *iv*=1, instrumental variables estimation with lagged variables as instruments. If *iv*=2, instrumental variables estimation with external instruments provided by matrix IVAR. If *iv*=3, fixed effects estimation with two dummies for each group, allowing for structural breaks. If iv=4, simple OLS estimation pooling all the data without fixed effects.

pl: Option toggle for obtaining a plot of the impulse responses (if *pl*=1).

IVAR: (TxN)xw matrix with the instruments, one in each column.

W: Weights for aggregating the historical decompositions, since we have a different one for each group.

d: Option toggle for obtaining (if *d*=1) the forecast error variance decomposition.

Outputs:

K1: Kx(KxP+1) matrix with the VAR coefficients. Each row corresponds to an equation of the VAR. The first column gives the constant terms. The next K columns correspond to the coefficients of the first lag, and so on up to P lags.

K2: (TxN)xK matrix with the residuals of the VAR. Each column corresponds to a different equation.

K3: KxK matrix with the covariance matrix of the residuals of the K equations.

K4: Kx(Kxit+1) matrix with the canonical moving average (MA) representation of the VAR. The variable *it* indicates the number of periods for which the MA is traced out, and it can be changed by modifying its value in the program *xmar.m* (which is described below). Its default value is 10. The first Kx1 column contains the constant terms, and the subsequent KxK matrices correspond to the values of the different lags, from 1 to it.

K5: Kx(Kxit+1) matrix with the orthogonalized MA representation of the VAR. It is achieved through a Choleski decomposition of the covariance matrix of the residuals. It is used as well as the impulse responses of the system to orthogonal shocks to the variables. The order of the variables is the same as in K4.

K6: (TxN)xK matrix with the orthogonalized residuals. Each column corresponds to a different equation.

K7: Kx(Kxit) matrix with the forecast error variance decomposition.

K8: Tx(KxK+K) matrix with the historical decomposition, as described below in *xhdec.m*.

K9: Kx(Kxit+1) matrix with the impulse responses of the variables of the system (in levels) to orthogonal shocks. The ordering of the responses is the same as in K4 and K5.

K10: Kx(Kxit) matrix with the standard error of the canonical MA representation. It does not include the standard error of the constant terms.

K11: Kx(Kxit) matrix with the standard error of the canonical MA representation in levels. It does not include the standard error of the constant terms.

K12: KxK matrix with the standard error of the asymptotic long-run response corresponding to the canonical MA representation in levels.

K13: Kx(Kxit) matrix with the standard error of the orthogonal MA representation. It does not include the standard error of the constant terms.

K14: Kx(Kxit) matrix with the standard error of the orthogonal MA representation in levels. It does not include the standard error of the constant terms.

K15: KxK matrix with the standard error of the asymptotic long run response corresponding to the orthogonal MA representation in levels.

Purpose:

It gives the standard errors of the canonical and orthogonal impulse responses of the VAR, and of its (infinite) long-run responses.

Format:

[K1,K2,K3,K4,K5,K6]=xvarse(A,K4,K3,Y,T)

Inputs:

A: Matrix with the coefficients of the VAR model. It corresponds to K1 in *xvarsec.m.*

K4: Matrix with the canonical MA representation of the VAR. It corresponds to matrix K4 in *xvarsec.m.*

K3: Covariance matrix of the residuals of the VAR. It corresponds to matrix K3 in *xvarsec.m.*

Y: (NxT)xK matrix with the variables of the system. It is the same input as G in *xvarsec.m.*

T: Number of time periods.

Outputs:

K1: Kx(Kxit+1) matrix with the standard errors of the canonical MA representation.

K2: Kx(Kxit+1) matrix with the standard errors of the canonical MA representation in levels.

K3: KxK matrix with the standard error of the asymptotic canonical impulse-response.

K4: Kx(Kxit) matrix with the standard errors of the orthogonal MA representation.

K5: Kx(Kxit) matrix with the standard errors of the orthogonal MA representation in levels.

K6: KxK matrix with the standard error of the asymptotic orthogonal impulse-response.

Purpose:

It performs the forecast error variance decomposition of the VAR, that is, the percentage of the forecast error of a variable explained by each orthogonal shock. It is used in *xvarsec.m*.

Format:

[K1]=xvardec(MA,d)

Inputs:

MA: Kx(Kxit+1) matrix with the orthogonal MA representation of the VAR. It is the output K5 in *xvarsec.m*.

d: Option toggle with two options. If *d*=1 it gives the variance decomposition in percentage terms. If *d*=0 it gives it in absolute quantities.

Outputs:

K1: Kx(Kxit) matrix containing for each period *it* a KxK matrix with the variance decomposition at that lag. In the KxK matrix, row entries indicate the responding variable and column entries indicate the shock.

Purpose:

It returns the canonical MA representation from the VAR coefficients. It is used by *xvarsec.m*.

Format:

[K1]=xmar(VAR,it)

Inputs:

VAR: Kx(Kxit+1) matrix with the coefficients of the VAR (equivalent to matrix K1 in *xvarsec.m*).

it: Number of lags for which we want the MA representation.

Outputs:

K1: Kx(Kxit+1) matrix with the canonical MA representation (equivalent to output K4 in *xvarsec.m*).

Purpose:

It cumulates the MA representation from a standard initial level of 1, such that it returns the impulse response of the variables in levels (for the case in which the VAR has been estimated with first differences).

Format:

[K1]=xmarlev(MA,W)

Inputs:

MA: Kx(Kxit+1) matrix with the MA representation.

W: 1xK vector of K options, one for each variable in the VAR. For those variables with a 1 in the corresponding column of this vector, the program gives the MA in levels. For those with a 0 it leaves the MA as it is. If there is no W vector then all impulse responses are in levels.

Outputs:

K1: Kx(Kxit+1) matrix with the impulse responses in levels. As always, the first column gives the intercepts and the subsequents KxK submatrices the MA representation at each lag.

xhdec.m *xhdec.m*

Purpose:

It performs the historical decomposition of the variables for the different orthogonal shocks.

Format:

[K1]=xhdec(MA,E,W,T1)

Inputs:

MA: Kx(Kxit+1) with the orthogonal MA representation (matrix K5 in *xvarsec.m*).

E: (NxT)xK matrix of the orthogonal residuals (matrix K6 in xvarsec).

W: (NxT)x1 matrix with the variable that weights the historical decompositions.

T1: Number of periods minus the number of lags, T-P.

Outputs:

K1: Tx(KxK+K) matrix with the historical decomposition. The different rows correspond to the time periods. The first K columns include the part of the first variable explained by each shock, from 1 to K. The following K columns contain the corresponding part of the second variable; and so on. The last K columns give the original variables.

Purpose:

It plots the MA representations as the impulse responses of the VAR, with their corresponding one standard error bands. It can be used either for the canonical or orthogonal MA, in levels or in differences.

Format:

xplotma(MA,S,ind1,ind2)

Inputs:

MA: Kx(Kxit+1) matrix with an MA representation (either K4, K5 or K9 in *xvarsec.m*).

S: Kx(Kxit) matrix with the corresponding standard errors, without the ones corresponding to the intercepts.

ind1 and ind2: Optional variables for choosing which impulse response we want from the possible KxK responses. The toggle *ind*1 indicates the number of the responding variable, and *ind*2 the number of the corresponding shock.

AUXILIARY PROGRAMS

This is the list of other *".m"* files that have been used in the main programs listed above. Some of them do very simple things (like pegging a vector of ones to a matrix or lagging the variables in a matrix several times), whereas some others perform whole parts of the main programs. Many of them perform an operation several times (for different groups), such that they are especially useful for manipulating panel data in general.

They are listed alphabetically with a brief description of what they do.

- *xdiff(A,T)*

  It differentiates the variables in all groups of matrix A, which is a panel with a variable in each column and N groups of T values each.

- *xdumols(H,T)*

  It performs multivariate OLS estimation with dummy variables for the intercept. Data are in matrix H, organized as usual, with the independent variable in the first column and the regressors in the remaining ones. It is used for the estimation of the VAR in *xvarsec.m.*

- *xdumols2(H,T1,T2)*

  This is similar to the previous one, but allows for two dummy variables to model a structural break (two periods of length T1 and T2, respectively). It is also used in *xvarsec.m.*

- *xdumxx.m; xdumxx2.m; xdumxy.m; xdumxy2.m*

  These four programs speed up the multiplication and inversion of matrices for *xdumols* and *xdumols2* when the number of dummy variables (and therefore the size of those matrices) is very large.

- *xkronese(X,N,P); xkroneye(X,N,P,Y); xkronp(X,a,b,Y); xkronxx(X,N,P,Y); xkronxp(X,N,P,Y); xkronxy(X,N,P,Y).*

  These programs are used for computing some large matrices needed for 2SLS estimation when the option of fixed effects or unrestricted coefficients between groups has been chosen.

In general they simplify matrix multiplication and kronecker products and speed up calculations.

- *xlag(A,p)*

  Takes a matrix A of order TxK and returns a matrix of order (TxK) with p lags for all the variables in the columns of A. The default value for p is 1.

- *xlags(A,p)*

  Takes a matrix A of order TxK and adjoints the same matrix lagged one period, then lagged two periods, and so on until p lags. The result is a matrix of order (T-p)x(Kxp). It is used for generating the regressors of a VAR model.

- *xlast(X,d)*

  It takes selected rows of matrix X. If d=1, it returns X without the first row. If d=2, it returns only even rows. If d=3, it takes uneven rows. If d=4, it takes only the last row. It is used for selecting the coefficients of interest when performing a regression.

- *xldiff(A,T)*

  A is a matrix with a panel data, with N groups of T periods each. This function takes each group and returns the growth rates of each column (i.e. each variable), by first differencing their logarithm.

- *xmatrix(m,d)*

  This function creates 3 special matrices described in the appendix of Luetkepohl (1991) and necessary for the calculation of the standard errors of the impulse-responses of a VAR.

- *xmeans(H,T)*

  It calculates from a data panel H the means and variances for all the variables of each group (output K1) and for all the panel variables as a whole (output K2).

- *xmed(X,T)*

  It transforms the variables in panel X for each group into deviations with respect to the mean.

- *xmsum(A)*

  A is a matrix of (KxK) x it, and this function sums all block matrices of size KxK. It is used for the calculation of the MA in levels.

- *xones(X,T)*

  It adds dummy variables to panel X, pegging the necessary columns of zeros and ones to the left of the matrix.

- *xpart(X,Y)*

  Partitioned multiplication (in blocks of 20x20) for the case of large matrices that cannot be handled with the PC version of MATLAB.

- *xpick(A,i,j)*

  A is the matrix of an MA or the impulse responses of a VAR. This function takes, for all periods, the response of the i_{th} variable to a shock in the j_{th} variable.

- *xq(X,T)*

  It removes the first observation in each group of panel X.

- *xstack(A,N)*

  It reorganizes a panel A with N groups and T periods by period blocks instead of group blocks. That is, the first N rows correspond to the observations of all groups in period 1, and so on.

- *xt0(K1); xt1(K1)*

  It gives the t-values for the null hypothesis that the coefficients of a regressions are, respectively, zero and one. The input $K1$ is a matrix with the coefficients in the first column and the standard errors in the second column.

- *xvec(A); xvech(A)*

  It performs the operators *vec* and *vech* as described in Lutkepohl (1988). It is used for the calculation of the standard errors of the impulse responses of a VAR.

- *xwhite(X,e,T,d)*

  This is the function that calculates the heteroskedasticity-robust standard errors in multivariate OLS or 2SLS. X is the matrix of the regressors, which in the instrumental variables case includes the instrumented regressors calculated in the first stage. The option d specifies if there are any constraints in the coefficients between groups: constrained (d=1), fixed effects (d=3) or unconstrained (d=2).

- *xwhitear(X,e,T,d,s)*

  This function is similar to the one before, but the robust standard errors will be robust for autocorrelation as well as heteroskedasticity. The first five options are the same as in the previous program. Option s input the order of autocorrelation of the residuals for which the standard errors will be robust.

Programs for data management and presentation

There are several programs that allow for the selection of specific variables from a dataset, with options to choose the time periods, the order of differences, and so on. Some other programs are used to create some new variables not included in the original dataset (like, for instance, real variables from the original nominal ones and the price indices).

Another set of programs are designed to create a useful presentation of the results. They put heading on columns, titles on tables and they generate tables in LATEX wordprocessing language.

Finally, another function *xagreg.m*, permits the aggregation of the variables in a panel by groups, with an option for geometric or arithmetic averages, and the posibility of weighting the aggregation with other variables as weights.

Index